THE CONTRIBUTORS

Project coordinator for this book is **Charles E. Cabell III,** an American who lives in Rome. Charles has been managing editor for Rome's English-language daily the *International Courier* and Rome correspondent for *Taxi* magazine.

The art essays, the Michelangelo tour of Rome, and the Cultural Timeline are the work of **Michael Hinden,** professor of English and Integrated Liberal Studies at the University of Wisconsin–Madison.

The architecture essays are by **Mary Beth Betts** and **Charles Ayes.** Mary Beth is an architectural historian teaching at the Cooper Union; Charles is an architect in New York.

Some information for the Traveler's Information section was compiled by **Taryn Schneider,** a writer whose credits include *Natural History* and *Travel Agent* magazines.

The vocabulary section was put together by **Giuseppe Manca,** who teaches Italian in New York.

The Business Brief is by **Sondra Snowdon,** author of *The Global Edge: How Your Company Can Win in the International Marketplace.*

The New York editor for the book is Debra Bernardi. Maps are by R.V. Reise and Verkehrsverlag, and Swanston Graphics.

A BANTAM TRAVEL GUIDE

ROME

1989

A QUICK & EASY GUIDE ™

BANTAM
NEW YORK ● TORONTO ● LONDON ● SYDNEY ● AUCKLAND

ROME 1989
A Quick and Easy Guide ™
A Bantam Book / April 1989

ISBN 0–553–34643–1

Published simultaneously in the United States and Canada

Bantam Books are published by Bantam Books, a division of
Bantam Doubleday Dell Publishing Group, Inc. Its trademark,
consisting of the words "Bantam Books" and the portrayal of
a rooster, is Registered in U.S. Patent and Trademark Office
and in other countries. Marca Registrada. Bantam Books, 666
Fifth Avenue, New York, New York 10103

PRINTED IN THE UNITED STATES OF AMERICA

0   9   8   7   6   5   4   3   2   1

CONTENTS

Tips on Getting the Most Out of This Guide

Bantam Travel Guides are designed to be extremely user friendly, but there are a few things you should know in order to get the maximum benefit from them.

1. You'll find a special **Travel Arrangements** section, easily identified by the black-bordered pages, toward the back of the book. This section can be invaluable in planning your trip.

2. The **Priorities** chapter will insure that you see and do the most important things when you visit your destination. Whether you're spending two days or two weeks there, you'll want to make the most of your time and certainly not miss the musts.

3. Note that in addition to our main selection of important restaurants you'll also find described in the text informal places to stop for lunch, a snack or a drink.

4. To help you instantly identify restaurant and hotel write-ups, whether they're in a list or mentioned in the text, we've designed the following two little versions of our friendly Bantam rooster. Miniatures of these roosters will appear at the beginning of restaurant and hotel lists and in the margin of the text whenever a restaurant or hotel is described there.

Restaurants

Hotels

1

TRAVELING IN ROME, 1989

Rome has to be eternal. What other city so severely and consistently tested has always managed to survive?

Motor vehicles are the scourge of the twentieth century. Over the past thirty years they have provoked more damage than nearly two thousand years of quakes, fires, plagues, looting, complacency, and pure quests for power. Modern Neroes fiddle through brief reigns as daily traffic throughout the metropolitan area increasingly paralyzes routine life, and creates the pollution that is crumbling ancient Rome's monuments. Municipal inadequacy and national inefficiency in dealing with the problem have created a quagmire to rival the marshland bogs where legend says that Romulus founded Rome on April 21, 753 B.C.

Archaeologists today are reassessing Rome's historical role in the development of the city-state. Until now, ancient Rome has been considered a military power that usurped the technical and cultural advancements of the Etruscans and Greeks; based on recent digs at the Palatine site that reputedly have uncovered ruins of the original village, scholars now believe Rome originated more than the civilization has been given credit for, and are reevaluating the cultural impact of ancient Rome.

Ancient Romans were convinced they were deified, preordained to rule the world. Their constant quest for conquest circled the Mediterranean in their effort to dominate the known world. Then came the invasions of Gaul and Britain, and all roads truly led to Rome, *caput mundi,* "capital of the world." The immense grandeur of the achievement has captivated the imagination of the centuries.

Charismatic politician-generals such as Julius Caesar and his great-nephew Octavius (who assumed the name Augustus as emperor) provided early leadership that is unknown in the petty politicking that disrupts Italy today. But in ensuing years, political feuds and plots corrupted the Empire, and it was divided into East and West. The papacy's political emergence forced hotly contested rivalry between imperialists, republicans, and papists. This continued throughout the Middle Ages, in the city-states of the warring Guelphs and Ghibellines.

In 1308 the papacy was forced to seek refuge in Avignon, France. It did not return to Rome until 1377, but even then there were rivals to Peter's throne. With the reign of Pope Alexander VI (Rodrigo Borgia), who freely wielded the sword of excommunication against any and all opponents who escaped the ire of his infamous offspring Cesare and Lucretia, Rome began to accumulate a powerful artistic patrimony through Alexander's patronage of such artists as Michelangelo, Raphael, and Bramante. Rome went on to become the baroque capital of the world with Urban VIII's commissioning of the architectural genius of Gianlorenzo Bernini and Borromini to revitalize Rome. Their artistic legacy is truly one of the beauties of the city.

The Risorgimento's unification of Italy under the House of Savoy in 1861 formally terminated the political power of the papacy. When Rome became capital of the Savoy kingdom in 1870, more subtle means of influence were applied to internal Italian affairs.

Boundaries were drawn with the 1922 Lateran Pact that established the Holy See as an independent state and achieved church recognition for the Fascist regime of Benito Mussolini.

The Vatican has undergone sharp criticism for its conduct during the Nazi occupation of Rome, especially for failure to intervene before the Fosse Ardeatine reprisal killings of 335 Italians. But individual acts of heroism were not rare. A brave Irish priest spirited a number of Allied aviators to freedom as well as the wife and son of the SS major who supervised the Fosse Ardeatine massacre.

During the occupation, Allied bombing of the San Lorenzo rail freight depot caused death and destruction among the civilian population, and forced a rare exit of then-Pope Pius XII from Vatican City.

Recently the streets of Rome have appeared more war-ravaged than following the city's liberation by the Allies in 1944, as the capital prepares for two major events. In 1990 Italy will host the World Cup soccer tournament, and in 1992 the final erasing of national barriers between European Economic Community nations is scheduled (the first steps toward European integration were signed in Rome on March 23, 1957). Hardly a street in Rome has escaped excavation to renovate and expand phone, gas, electric, water, and sewer lines to handle the expected crowds. With time-tested lack of coordination seemingly inherent in Italian bureaucracy, repeated street closings have added to the already desperate traffic snarl in Rome, complicated by the constant and abrupt reversal of the direction of one-way streets. And contractors live in constant fear of uncovering artifacts of archaeological significance: the Fine Arts Commission will then block all work—sometimes for months—pending a decision on the fate of the new find.

The same bureaucratic neglect has dogged the effort to save Rome's crumbling architectural heritage. The first-century Arch of Constantine has remained under scaffolding erected for renovation seven years ago. Work on the Palace of Justice took so long that grass grew on the scaffolding. And yet much of Rome's charm lies in its cavalier attitude toward its own greatness.

This cavalier attitude unfortunately can show up as a lack of courtesy and civic pride. Service in downtown shops can be appalling. One Rome daily newspaper was prompted to run a clerk of the week contest; the effect was totally undetectable. Sales personnel snarl today as beautifully as they did yesterday.

The dream of every neighborhood is that a local resident will be elected mayor. This will assure that their streets are properly lit, that garbage will be collected daily and the streets swept at least once a week. Impersonality has taken its toll as condominium lifestyles trade simplicity for modern convenience.

The southernization of Rome has taken its toll, manning the lethargic bureaucracy less common in the industrious, Austro-Hungarian-influenced north. (Southern Italy was controlled by the Bourbons who reigned at a maximum level of exploitation, giving nothing in return. After the Bourbons, the popular attitude saw the state as the goose that laid the golden egg, with everyone entitled to as many as they could wrangle.)

Leftist labor laws have greatly restricted private employers and state supervisors. The former maintain an institutional independence; the latter are tied to political nepotism with overtones of Third World mentality. Under such circumstances, providing adequate and accurate tourist assistance is a real catch-22, and without tourism Rome and its entrepreneurs would be in dire straits.

Don't be scared off; forewarned is forearmed, and the objective—the Eternal City—is worth your patience. Not all Rome's inhabitants are gruff, indifferent, or hustling—after all, they are Italians. The city can be amazingly hospitable; much can depend on the visitor. Therein lies the secret to a successful Roman holiday: proper perspective, and a share in the admiration of the ages for this decadent queen of cities. At times it may resemble Looney Tunes, but it's not Disney World.

2

ORIENTING YOURSELF

Where to start is the real Roman dilemma. Unlike other great cities in Italy, Rome's major attractions are so many and so widely dispersed that it is impossible to see them all by foot in a limited amount of time. To simplify the task, think of Rome as three general areas: the Vatican, monumental Rome, and archaeological Rome.

The Vatican includes the Basilica of St. Peter's, the Vatican Museums (including the Sistine Chapel and the Raphael Rooms), and the papal fortress of Castel Sant'Angelo. For purposes of simplification, we're also considering the residential Prati area nearby as part of the Vatican area. The Vatican area is across the Tiber, directly west of the center of modern downtown Rome. It is easily accessible by the subway A line (Ottaviano, the last stop); the number 30 tram (Piazza Risorgimento, the last stop), which makes one long sweep around most of central Rome; and the number 64 bus, which terminates its run in the shadow of the colonnades embracing St. Peter's Square. (The number 64 line runs from the central Termini train station through the heart of Rome—Via Nazionale, Piazza Venezia, and Corso Vittorio Emanuele II.)

Monumental Rome is the area of palaces and monuments on both sides of the central Via del Corso from Piazza del Popolo to Piazza Venezia. It is bounded on the west by the Tiber, and on the east by the Pincio area, down Trinita dei Monti to the Spanish Steps, and along Via Sistina to Piazza Barberini. This area is well-serviced by the A line, with stops at Piazza Barberini, Piazza di Spagna, and Piazzale Flaminio (just outside Piazza del Popolo).

Most of this area is a pedestrian island; only public vehicles and those with special permits are allowed. Sundays and holidays are the best for daytime visits, since traffic will be reduced to a bare minimum. Most of the area is especially attractive in the evening, when the illuminated sights seem even more impressive.

This area is also the main shopping area, offering pleasant distractions and no lack of places for a snack or refreshment. Distances shrink amazingly when traveling by foot, since major monuments, churches, and fountains are never more than five minutes apart.

The concentration of sights becomes more intensive heading down the Corso toward the archaeological area, the excavations of what was once ancient Rome. The monumental area ends in Piazza del Campidoglio, the square designed by Michelangelo atop the Capitoline Hill, offering a balcony view over the major ancient ruins, with the Colosseum as a backdrop.

To reach **archaeological Rome,** take the street downhill east, from the Campidoglio to Via dei Fori Imperiali, which leads directly to the Colosseum, across from the entrance to the Roman Forum and Palatine Hill. This is the heart of ancient Rome, once ruler of the Mediterranean world. Interesting mosaic maps on the embankment walls along the right side of Via dei Fori Imperiali illustrate the expansion of the Roman Empire.

To the left, across the street from the Colosseum, is the B line metro stop, the most convenient means for reaching the archaeological area. Up the hill behind the Colosseum are numerous bus and tram stops, including the number 118 bus to the Via Appia Antica and the Catacombs. The most interesting are San Calisto and San Sebastiano; since the catacombs alternate closing days, one of these is always open.

Between the two catacombs, on Via delle Sette Chiese, is the Fosse Ardeatine site where more than three hundred Italians were executed in tufo caves on direct orders from Hitler after a German police patrol was bombed in the center of Rome. An impressive monument marks the site.

As part of a visit to archaeological Rome, you can make a sidetrip to San Giovanni in Laterano (the cathedral of Rome) and the Holy Stairs, just off the A line stop at the beginning of the modern Via Appia.

Beyond this basic breakdown of the major sights in Rome are the following:

- The complex in front of Stazione **Termini** includes the church of Santa Maria degli Angeli and Diocletian's Baths, housing the National Roman Museum. The basilica of Santa Maria Maggiore is also near the rail terminal, just off the B line.
- **Trastevere,** meaning "across the Tiber," is basically the area between the Tiber and Gianicolo hill. Once considered the last bastion of "true" Romans, the area was discovered by expatriates who considered it quaint. Prices soared, places were renovated, and it is no longer quite so quaint—with residents that include royalty and some of the world's wealthiest individuals. It is still known as a good dining area, with a number of trattorias and restaurants for all tastes and price ranges, even though fast food and foreign fare have encroached on the previously purely Roman domain. The area of the Sunday flea market, Trastevere is also the site of the church of Santa Maria in Trastevere, only a five-minute walk from Piazza Sonnino on Viale di Trastevere. The area is accessible by the number 280 bus from Prati and the Vatican, and the number 710, 718, and 719 buses which have terminals in the Piazza Venezia area. Immediately north of Piazza Sonnino are **Tiberina Island** and the main synagogue on Lungotevere de'Cenci in the old **ghetto.**
- The **Borghese area** lies north of the city center. Consider a brief tour of the Galleria Borghese, Modern Art Gallery, and Villa Giulia Etruscan museum, which edge the north and east of the largest park in Rome, Villa Borghese, which also contains the

Rome zoo. **Pincio** is another park area; the "balcony of Rome," it overlooks Piazza del Popolo and extends into Villa Borghese. The **Parioli** area borders Villa Borghese on the north. There are a number of embassies here, as well as the official residence of the U.S. ambassador.

The **Via Veneto,** running south from Villa Borghese, is no longer the street of *La Dolce Vita.* Today, hookers must compete with tourists for space on the streets, and the major attractions are some good restaurants and shopping.

3

TRANSPORTATION

TIMING YOUR VISIT

Travel itineraries should be carefully planned to avoid co-inciding with major religious and national holidays, when many doors are closed in Rome. This is particularly true during the week between Christmas and the New Year, when Dec. 26 is also a holiday in Italy. Since banks also close, changing currency is also affected.

The Holy Week between Palm Sunday and Easter is the busiest single period of the year for Rome hotels: advance reservations are essential. This is generally considered the beginning of the tourist season, but if Easter is early things can slacken in mid-April.

Two big Italian holidays are April 25—Liberation Day—and May 1. If either falls on a Friday or a Monday, expect great difficulty in booking a room without advance reserva-tions; Italians will flood Rome for the long weekend.

July and August can be the most uncomfortable months to visit Rome; for the past three years the heat has been rivaled only by the humidity. September and October are increasingly favored by Italians and Northern Europeans for visits to Rome. The onslaught of Scandinavian and German school groups at the end of September and be-ginning of October can fill the more economical hotels, creating an overflow into the better categories that can make it impossible to book a room on arrival. Reservations are always a good idea.

Rome has three airports, seven state-run rail terminals and three private rail depots. Provincial bus service is based at depots throughout the city; there are two subway lines and an extensive city bus system. Despite all this, transportation is clogged and traffic heavy.

Rome is rapidly being strangled by automobile traffic that city authorities seem unequipped to regulate. And despite the numerous services and depots available, ninety percent of rail and air traffic is concentrated on Stazione Termini and Leonardo da Vinci (Fiumicino) Airport.

ARRIVING IN ROME

Leonardo da Vinci is the official name of Rome's international airport near the small port town of Fiumicino. This can create confusion for the traveler, since abroad the airport is referred to as da Vinci, while in Rome it is always **Fiumicino.** (It also explains why some identification tags on luggage destined for Rome read FCO.)

The international and domestic terminals at Fiumicino are side by side. The airport information number is (06) 60121; information is available in English, and the switchboard can transfer calls to all airlines. Most airline offices in Rome are in the area between Via Veneto, Via Barberini, and Via Bissolati. All are closed noon Sat.–9 A.M. Mon.

Only Alitalia has a 24-hour, seven-day-a-week all-service number: (06) 5456. You can't reach other airlines (for reservations, confirmation, etc.) during the weekend.

Bus service from the airport to Termini Station is Lit. 5,000 per person. The 22-mile ride takes 45 min., traffic permitting; buses leave from Termini's Via Giolitti Air Terminal, and from both the international and domestic terminals at Fiumicino, every 15 min. 7 A.M.–9 P.M. and every 30 min. 9 P.M.–7 A.M. There are train, bus, and subway connections at Termini.

Once the Rome airport, **Ciampino** is now basically a military facility that handles charters and acts as a backup for Fiumicino in bad weather. (Being close to the coast, Fiumicino is more likely to be subject to rare fogs.) The Ciampino information number is (06) 724241; information is available in Italian only.

Besides taxi, the best means of reaching Rome from Ciampino is to take the ACOTRAL bus from the airport to the Anagnina subway (metro) stop, then take the A line (in the direction of Ottaviano) into Rome.

Having lire with you on arrival is a must at Ciampino; there are no banking facilities. Designed more to accommodate bank employees than international travelers, limited banking is available at Fiumicino.

When leaving from Fiumicino, if you want to exchange lire for the currency of your next destination, you must present a foreign-exchange slip from a Rome bank as proof that an official lire transaction was originally made.

Airport taxis are assigned to Fiumicino and Ciampino for two-week stints. Cabs assigned to the airport cannot work in the city, and vice versa. This obliges cabs to return to the airport empty, at the original passenger's expense. A run to Fiumicino thus has Lit. 14,000 added to the meter fare; from Fiumicino to the city, the added fee is Lit. 10,000. The taxi ride will total around Lit. 50,000, not including extra cost for luggage. To and from Ciampino the added fee is Lit. 7,000 (with total cost around Lit. 40,000).

TRAIN CONNECTIONS

Trains from the main Rome station of Termini connect Italy's capital with the rest of the country as well as Western and Eastern European destinations. Information can be obtained from the English-language information counter in the station at Piazza dei Cinquecento, or by telephoning (06) 4775 (in Italian only).

Other Rome train stations are:

Ostiense, Piazzale Partigiani, tel. (06) 5750732 (connections to Ostia, Viterbo, Naples via Formia, and Nettuno)

Prenestina, Piazzale della Stazione Prenestina, tel. (06) 272072 (to Avezzano and Pescara)

San Pietro, Via Stazione San Pietro, tel. (06) 631391 (to Viterbo via la Storta)

Tiburtina, Circonvallazione Nomentana, tel. (06) 4956626 (to Ancona via Foligno, Florence, Bologna, Naples via Formia, Pescara via Avezzano, Nettuno, Velletri, and Viterbo)

Trastevere, Piazzale Biondo, tel. (06) 5816076 (to Genoa via Pisa, Nettuno, and Viterbo)

Tuscolana, Via Mestre, tel. (06) 7576359 (to Naples via Formia, and Nettuno).

There also are three local train services under ACOTRAL, with departure points at Piazzale Flaminio (connections to Civita Castellana and Viterbo, plus an urban link to Parioli's Piazza Euclide); Roma Laziali, on Via Giolitti behind Termini; and Porta San Paolo, across the street from the Pyramid metro stop (connections to Ostia Lido and Ostia

Antica, every 30 min. 5:30 A.M.–midnight). An hourly bus service to Ostia substitutes for the trains after midnight. For ACOTRAL information call (06) 57531.

BUS CONNECTIONS

ACOTRAL's extraurban blue buses serve the province of Rome and other key points in Lazio. Depots are along the metro lines, thereby offering fast and easy connections between provincial bus lines and inner-city destinations.

ACOTRAL information can be obtained from the main office, Via Ostiense 131; tel. (06) 57531. Buses depart from Via Castro Pretorio, Viale Giulio Cesare (Lepanto metro stop), the EUR-Fermi metro station, Piazza dei Cinquecento (in front of the Termini FS station), Piazzale Flaminio (just outside Piazza del Popolo), Via Gaeta (near Termini), Via Giolitti (the Termini departure point for da Vinci-Fiumicino airport), Piazza M. Fanti, Piazza di Cinecittà, and the Pyramid (Piramide) metro stop.

PUBLIC TRANSPORTATION WITHIN THE CITY

The Roman's near-masochistic sense of individualism manifests itself in the insistence on driving in inner Rome, most of which is banned to private autos except for those of residents, merchants, and such friends of city hall who have acquired permanent windshield permits. Traffic often paralyzes what could otherwise be an efficient transit system. This makes the Metropolitana (subway) much more efficient than surface transportation. The metro is also the spine of the urban transportation system; a number of city bus lines terminate at or near metro stops.

State tourist board (EPT) information offices at the turnpike stations Roma Nord and Roma Sud, the international airport (da Vinci-Fiumicino), and Termini (a kiosk at track number 3) provide free city maps of principal bus, tram, and metro routes.

The metro is run by ACOTRAL, which also operates provincial bus service; city buses are run by ATAC.

TAKING THE SUBWAY

The two metro lines are simply designated A and B. Direction is indicated by the terminals at the end of each line. The A and B lines intersect under Termini train station. You can change lines without paying another fare. The fare is Lit. 700 per ride regardless of distance. Booklets of ten tickets may be purchased at the reduced rate of Lit. 6,000. These may be purchased at most underground stops; those not equipped with vendor booths have coin-operated vending machines. For information call (06) 57531.

The A line runs from Ottaviano (200 yards from the Vatican) to Anagnina, at the base of the Albani Hills. The A line travels under Viale Giulio Cesare, crosses the Tiber, cuts under the heart of monumental Rome with stops at Piazzale Flaminio (with a pedestrian tunnel to Piazza del Popolo), Piazza di Spagna (with a pedestrian tunnel and walk to Via Veneto), Piazza Barberini, and Piazza della Repubblica (at the top of Via Nazionale) before arriving under Termini. The A line continues to the large open-air market at Piazza Vittorio, then to San Giovanni at the beginning of the Via Appia (near the St. John Lateran Basilica). The A proceeds under Via Appia to Colli Albani, where it veers under the Via Tuscolana and on to Cinecittà (the Hollywood-on-the-Tiber film studios) before terminating at Anagnina.

The B line, from EUR (east of Rome on the way to Ostia) to Termini, is being expanded. It now runs from Termini to Cavour (near Santa Maria Maggiore), to the Colosseum (Colosseo), Circo Massimo (Circus Maximus, in front of the U.N.'s Food and Agriculture Organization), and Piramide (near the local terminal for Ostia Lido). Eventually the line will run to Ostiense train station, with a connection to Fiumicino airport to be run by the state railroad.

TAKING THE BUS OR TRAM

ACOTRAL ticket vendors sell a daily BIG ticket (Lit. 2,400) valid for 24 hours on both metro and all city bus and tram (ATAC) lines. This is the only bus-tram-metro ticket combination.

The city transit company (ATAC) issues regular monthly one-line and multi-line passes for residents. For tourists, a weekly multi-line pass (Lit. 10,000) is available at the ATAC kiosk in front of Termini, in Piazza dei Cinquecento. As are all urban buses in Italy, ATAC buses and trams are yellow.

Individual tickets for trams and buses are purchased at newsstands and tobacco counters near ATAC stops for Lit. 700 each, or Lit. 6,000 for a booklet of ten. Ticket holders board at the back of the bus or tram, and must cancel tickets in the machine to the left of the aisle. Pass holders board at the front of the bus or tram. Everyone exits through the center door.

Ottaviano • Lepanto • Flaminio • Spagna • Barberini • Repubblica • Termini

Via Cavour

Colosseo

Circo Massimo

Piramide

Garbatella

San Paolo

Magliana

Eur Marconi

Eur Fermi

Laurentina

Vittorio Emanuele

Manzoni

San Giovanni

Re di Roma

Ponte Lungo

Furio Camillo

Colli Albani

Acro di Travertino

Porta Furba

Numidio Quadrato

Lucio Sestio

Giulio Agricola

Subaugusta

Cinecittà

Anagnina

ROME METRO

Company inspectors regularly patrol city routes. Anyone found without a properly cancelled ticket will be fined Lit. 10,000 on the spot. Keep this in mind if you feel like doing as the Romans do and don't buy a ticket.

TAXIS

Taxis are an interesting undertaking in Rome—which is our polite way of saying you should watch what you're doing. All legitimate taxis are yellow. No licensed cab driver will approach anyone at train stations and airports offering his services. Legitimate cabs are in line in front of terminals, often under the watchful eye of a city policeman. At the air terminal less scrupulous drivers sometimes will exploit jet lag and travelers' unfamiliarity with Rome and Italian currency. If the driver refuses to turn on his meter, ask him to stop; call a policeman; or sit back, enjoy the ride, and refuse to pay upon reaching your destination— but be prepared for a screaming match, and call the local police precinct.

When a meter is turned on, a starting fee is registered. If a cab has been called from an outdoor stand or radio taxi co-op, the driver turns on his meter for the drive to the pickup point, and the meter will be running on arrival. There is a flat Lit. 3,000 night fee in effect 10 P.M.–7 A.M., added onto the meter fee. The same is done on Sundays and holidays. There is no such thing as a per passenger charge, but there is a charge for each piece of baggage. All taxi regulations should be available on a printed fare sheet under the seal of the city of Rome in each and every yellow cab.

When tipping, round off to the next highest thousand, or empty your pockets of change. But use your own discretion when deciding how deserving your driver is.

DRIVING

Regardless of what has been written and said about Rome traffic, nothing can match the initial impact. The only relief is in August, when fools rush in where angels fear to tread. Most of a broiling city has been deserted for the annual holiday, which means very little traffic and an abundance of usually nonexistent parking. But try to find a restaurant, dry cleaner, or laundry, and then you'll know who went on vacation.

Rome is surrounded by a beltway indicated by green turnpike signs reading "GRA" (Grande Raccordo Anulare). All turnpikes and major roads to Rome are linked to this ring road, which can help drivers avoid much grief if they arrive in Rome on the opposite side of the city from their final destination.

Clockwise around the beltway arrival routes are:

SS3 Via Flaminia (due north)

SS4 Via Salaria

The A1 Rome–Milan turnpike approach road to Roma Nord

SS5 Via Tiburtina (to Tivoli)

the A24 Rome–L'Aquila

SS6 Via Casilina (to Palestrina)

the A2 Rome-Naples approach road for Roma Sud

SS215 Via Tuscolana (for Frascati and the Albani Hills)

SS7 Via Appia (passing Ciampino and the lakes of Castel Gandolfo and Nemi en route to Naples)

SS148, practically due south of the city, which is an extension of Via Cristoforo Colombo, which pierces EUR (this is the road for the industrial zone at Pomezia en route to Latina, San Felice Circeo, and the Terracina ferry port for the island of Ponza)

SS201, the main route to Fiumicino, southwest of Rome, with a turnoff that becomes the A12 to Civitavecchia

SS1 Via Aurelia, due west, entering Rome behind the Vatican (connecting with the Circonvallazione Cornelia, crossing the Via Olimpica inner loop, and arriving at the Tiber on Via Gregorio VII: then chaos reigns)

SS2 Via Cassia (to Siena), running northwest and completing the GRA loop

The Cassia and Casilina are the worst roads to use to enter Rome. The best are the Colombo, Salaria, and Flaminia, in that order. Try to arrive between 2 and 4 P.M. Mon.–Sat. and between 10 A.M. and 6 P.M. Sun. Otherwise rush-hour and end-of-the weekend traffic is impossible.

CAR RENTALS

Auto rental facilities are available in Rome, but tourists beginning their travels in Rome should forget the convenience factor of picking up an automobile at the airport and weigh it against the inconvenience of major traffic snarls en route to a hotel in Rome. For touring Rome, cars are an invitation to frustration. Main one-way streets change directions seemingly at whim, adding to the chaos.

Roma

ss 2 — Siena — ss 3 — Mentana
Via Cassia — Prima Porta — ss 4 — Settebagni
la Giustiniana — 2 — A14 — 4
9 — 2 — Via Salaria — 5 — G.R.A.
Ottavia — Via Flaminia — M. Sacro — L'Aquila
S. Onofrio — 12 — 3 — Via Tiburtina
G.R.A. — 11 — Tor Sapienza — Napoli
CITTÀ D. VATICANO — 1 — Centocelle
Via Aurelia — 10 — 13 — Cine città — A2
ss 1 — 3 — Garba-tella — Via Casilina — 3
4 — Magliana — 14 — Via Prenestina — ss 215
Civitavecchia, Genova — 7 — 1 — 6 — EUR — Ciampino — Frascati
Leonardo da Vinci (Fiumicino) — Via Appia Nuova — 4 — Ciampino — ss 7
Acilia — 2 — 1 — G.R.A. — 2
Ostia Antica — Via del Mare — Spinaceto — 4
ss 8 bis — Via C. Colombo — ss 148
Lido di Ostia — Lanna
0 — 10 — 20 km

N

ROME

| 0 | Kilometers | 20 |
| | Miles | 12.4 |

© RV Reise - und Verkehrsverlag, München

These are the best international organizations, plus two reliable national agencies:

Leonardo da Vinci–Fiumicino: (International terminal) Avis, tel. (06) 601579; Europcar, tel. (06) 601879, telex 614564; Hertz, tel. (06) 601241, telex 610201; Maggiore, tel. (06) 601678. (National terminal) Avis, tel. (06) 601531; Europcar, tel. (06) 601977; Hertz, tel. (06) 601553; Maggiore, tel. (06) 601508.

Ciampino Airport: Avis, tel. (06) 6001955; Europcar, tel. (06) 7240387; Hertz, tel. (06) 600095; Maggiore, tel. (06) 7240368.

Rome: Avis, Via Sardegna 38A; tel. (06) 4701229. Europcar, Via Lombardia 7; tel. (06) 465802; telex 612358. Hertz, Via Salustiana 28; tel. (06) 463334; telex 621068. Maggiore, Via Po 8A; tel. (06) 858696. Prestige, Via Marco Aurelio 47B; tel. (06) 732542; telex 620889.

To avoid Saturday afternoon and Sunday pickup and return problems, clear your plans in advance; the car rental firms normally close their offices at these times. Alternative arrangements are possible.

BIKE RENTALS

It is possible to tour Rome by bicycle. Rentals are available at the exit of the Piazza di Spagna A line metro stop. Fees are Lit. 3,000 an hour or Lit. 10,000 for an entire day (9 A.M.–midnight). To obtain a bike you must leave an identity card or passport on deposit to assure the bike's return. If you value your life you'll limit bike riding to the city's pedestrian island, between Piazza di Spagna and Via del Corso, and Piazza del Popolo and Via del Tritone.

4

PRIORITIES

It's difficult to imagine needing less than three days to see just the basics of Rome. One day is required to visit the Vatican, its museums, and Castel Sant'Angelo. Another day can be exhausted touring the fountains, monuments, and churches in monumental old Rome. Archaeological Rome can be just as demanding, with the Colosseum, the Roman Forum, and many other important ruins.

Fortunately, you can sightsee at night, taking pleasant evening strolls around the Trevi Fountain, the Pantheon, and Piazza Navona, where there is pleasant caffè life and a number of good restaurants.

Since the Colosseum and Forum can easily be seen on the same day, tour this area any day other than Tuesday, when the Forum is closed, and include the church of San Clemente on your tour, just a ten-minute stroll behind the Colosseum on Piazza San Clemente, between Via Labicana and Via San Giovanni in Laterano.

The following sights should be on any list of things to see and do in Rome. The order is alphabetical; decide for yourself what to do first. Sights are keyed in to areas of Rome, as well as to the color map of the city at the back of the book. In the neighborhood key, reference is made to the page number of the color insert and the appropriate map coordinates.

Baths of Caracalla (Terme di Caracalla)

ARCHAEOLOGICAL ROME, P. 7, D5

These second-century baths were among the largest and most important in ancient Rome. Open-air opera is staged here in summer. Acoustics are poor, so vie for central seats, but bring a sweater—even the warmest summer can have cool nights. For information on the opera call the Teatro dell'Opera, telephone (06) 461755; or Caracalla, (06) 5758300. The baths are open Tuesday through Saturday 9 A.M. to 6 P.M., to 1 P.M. Sunday and Monday. Take the number 118 bus from behind the Colosseum or the number 90 bus from the center of Rome; you can stop here on your way to the Catacombs.

Nearby: The Circus Maximus, once used for chariot races, is northwest of the baths. A five-minute walk away is the medieval Santa Marie in Cosmedin Church and the Bocca della Verita (mouth of truth); legend has it anyone putting their hand in the Bocca (an ancient drain cover sculpted as a face) will lose it if telling a lie.

Capitol (Campidoglio)

MONUMENTAL ROME, P. 6, D3

The Piazza del Campidoglio, designed by Michelangelo, sits at the top of Capitoline Hill. To the left of the square is the Church of Santa Maria d'Aracoeli, with frescoes by Pinturicchio. Facing each other are the Palazzo Nuovo and Palazzo dei Conservatori, now the Capitoline Museums. The Nuovo houses mainly classical statues; the Conservatori features a picture gallery, with famous works such as Caravaggio's *John the Baptist.* The museums are open 9 A.M. to 2 P.M. Tuesday through Friday; to 11:30 P.M. on Saturday; to 1 P.M. on Sundays and holidays; also from 5 to 8 P.M. on Tuesdays and Thursdays. Telephone 6782862 to confirm days and hours. Behind the Campidoglio, there's a wonderful view of the Colosseum and Roman Forum.

Castel Sant'Angelo

VATICAN, PP. 1/2, B2

First completed in A.D. 139 as the emperor Hadrian's tomb, the Castel was converted into a citadel because of its strategic position on the Tiber. The Ponte

Sant'Angelo crossing the river in front of the Castel once led to a drawbridge at the entrance of the fort. The moat around Castel Sant'Angelo was fed by the Tiber's waters, but the road running parallel to the river makes this difficult to imagine now.

The **bronze statue of the angel** atop the castle has just returned by helicopter from extensive restoration. It represents a vision received by St. Gregory at the end of a 6th-century plague. When the statue was first erected the fortress was renamed Sant'Angelo. In the 9th century Pope Leo IV walled in the Vatican and surrounding area up to the castle, which became a fortified residence. There is a passageway (the Passetto) atop the walls that connects the castle with Vatican City.

The citadel has been modified by several popes. A number of interesting **papal apartments and galleries** may be visited; **medieval arms** are also on display. The top of the castle affords a fine view. It was from this point that Puccini had his *Tosca* leap to her death.

The Castel is on Lungotevere Castello, across the Tiber from downtown Rome. Take the A line metro, the number 30 tram, or the number 64 bus.
Nearby: St. Peter's Square and Basilica; the Vatican Museums.

Catacombs ARCHAEOLOGICAL ROME

These underground Christian cemeteries line the ancient Appian Way, Via Appia Antica. You can see tombs of various sizes, chapels that have been carved out of the rock, and early examples of Christian carvings and paintings on the walls. Two of the best known are San Calisto, at number 110, and San Sebastiano, at number 136. Tours are available in English. Open 8:30 A.M. to noon and 2:30 to 5:30 P.M., to 5 P.M. in winter. Take the number 118 bus from behind the Colosseum.

Colosseum ARCHAEOLOGICAL ROME, P. 7, D4

At the end of Via dei Fori Imperiali is the most imposing reminder of ancient Rome, the Colosseum (open 9 A.M. to 3:30 P.M. in winter, to 7 P.M. in summer, to 1 P.M. Sunday and holidays). Begun by Vespasian in A.D. 72

during the Flavian dynasty, it is also known as the Flavian Amphitheater. It was completed by Titus in A.D. 80,
when festivities lasted for one hundred days. The four-
tiered arena could accommodate 50,000 spectators at
its gladiator combats, "hunts," and mock sea battles.
Much of the Colosseum's deterioration was due to its
use as a quarry in the mid-15th century. Stone and marble were removed for the construction of St. Peter's,
the Palazzo di Venezia, Palazzo della Cancelleria, and
the Ripetta river port (once on the Tiber near Piazza
del Popolo), among other structures.

In modern times, pollution has caused more damage
in thirty years than stone-looting, quakes, fire, and foreign invasion had in nearly two thousand years. During
extensive restoration at the outset of the 1980s, interesting areas were uncovered in a lower level beneath
the arena that give further insight into the operation of
the Colosseum (they're open 9 A.M. to noon, Tuesday
through Saturday).

The B line metro stops across the street.

Nearby: The Roman Forum; the Palatine Hill; and the
bus to the Catacombs (the Baths of Caracalla are along
the way).

Palatine Hill   ARCHAEOLOGICAL ROME, PP. 6/7, D4

Romulus and Remus were said to have been found on
this hill, once covered with public buildings and homes
of prominent Romans. Highlights include the House of
Livia, the Palace of the Flavians, and the baths of Septimus Severus. Open 9 A.M. to 7 P.M., to 5 P.M. in winter.
Take the B line metro to the Colosseum.

Nearby: The Colosseum; the Roman Forum.

Pantheon   MONUMENTAL ROME, P. 2, C3

Standing on Piazza della Rotonda, this is the most complete building remaining from Imperial Rome. Originally
constructed in about 27 B.C., it was rebuilt by the Emperor Hadrian around 118–125. A temple to the gods
as well as a symbol of Hadrian's power, the structure
is especially impressive because of its dome, wider than

that of St. Peter's. There is active nightlife in the area, so an evening visit is a good idea.

At one point the square in front of the Pantheon was surfaced with wood that was a gift from the Argentine. (Argentina). According to old-timers the wood diminished the noise of passing carriages, which disturbed the nobility, wealthy merchants, and clergy who resided in the area.

An Italian fast-food eatery is behind the **obelisk,** placed here in 1711 by Pope Clement XI. Redecorated with dolphins and the pope's coat of arms, the original obelisk dates to the sixth century B.C. and bears hieroglyphic inscriptions that mention Ramses II. A similar **obelisk** stands in nearby Piazza della Minerva (to the left of the Pantheon), on a marble elephant base by a pupil of Bernini. It stands in front of **Santa Maria sopra Minerva** church, which was founded in the eighth century on the remains of a temple to Minerva and rebuilt in Gothic style in the 12th. The facade was rebuilt and the interior redone during the Renaissance.

You can take the A line metro and walk from Piazza di Spagna; the number 119 tram passes through Piazza Rotonda; you can also take bus number 90 or 70. **Nearby:** The Trevi Fountain and Piazza Navona.

Just up Via della Maddalena is the **Caffè delle Palme,** offering one of the widest selections of home-made *gelati* in Rome. In the back is a video bar for youngsters. Around the corner to the right is **Giolitti,** at Via Uffici del Vicario 40, which serves its giant sundaes until 2 A.M.

South of the Pantheon, towards the Torre Argentina on Via del Torre Argentina, in little more than a hole in the wall at number 20 is **Pascucci,** the home of the best fruit shakes in the city. Though not strictly a warm-weather drink, these can be especially refreshing during torrid summer months.

West of the Pantheon, in Piazza Sant'Eustachio at number 82 is the **Sant'Eustachio** caffè, noted for its creamy espresso coffee. If you're a cappuccino buff you won't find any place in Italy that can top this. If you don't want it sweetened say so when ordering, as sugar is auto-

The Pantheon
(around 27 B.C.; A.D. 118–125)

No one knows exactly how the Pantheon was constructed. Legends tell of a mountain of earth supporting the dome as the liquid concrete hardened and set. The Emperor Hadrian, according to these tales, had this mound sprinkled with gold to ensure its removal. Even standard wood scaffolding seems unlikely. Nevertheless, the Pantheon pairs innovative construction with spectacular form.

Surprisingly, the unusual interior of this Roman monument has a rather traditional temple exterior in front. A rectangular vestibule masks the circular shape of the building on the exterior. Within, the building is a domed cylinder 143 feet high awash with color and light. On sunny days the open round window (oculus) of the roof projects a moving beam of sunlight into the interior. On rainy days a column of water and light streams into the center of the space. Alternating recessed niches and projecting shrines sculpturally define the ground level. Above this, a portion of the original paneled band of richly colored marbles can still be seen, over the niche to the right of the central apse. The space culminates in the coffered dome with its open oculus.

Rebuilt by the Emperor Hadrian over a 27 B.C. structure by Agrippa, the Pantheon was both a temple to all the gods and a sign of Hadrian's political power. The building's harmony of form produced a potent symbol of the spiritual unity of the cosmos and the worldly order of the Roman Empire.

—Mary Beth Betts and Charles Ayes

matically added to both espresso and cappuccino here. Don't be bashful, or you'll never make it through the crowds to the bar.

Piazza Sant'Eustachio is behind the Italian **Senate.** Across the square, in a courtyard beside the Senate is an old **Roman tub** found during excavation to expand Senate facilities just a few years ago. Now a fountain, it is especially picturesque when illuminated in the evening.

Piazza del Popolo

MONUMENTAL ROME,
P. 2, C1

The entrance to the city is the third-century Porta del
Popolo, adorned by Bernini. The church of Santa Maria
del Popolo contains frescoes by Pinturicchio and two
masterpieces by Caravaggio, *The Conversion of St. Paul*
and the *Crucifixion of St. Peter*. The obelisk in the center of the piazza was taken from an Egyptian sun temple
and brought to Rome for the Circus Maximus. Take the
A line metro to Flaminio.

Nearby: There is good shopping along Via del Babuino
to Piazza di Spagna.

 At opposite sides of the square are the well-known **Rosa-
ti** (just completely renovated, amid cries of scandal when
it was rumored that the new tenant would be McDonald's)
and **Canova** caffès, gathering spots to see and at which
to be seen.

Piazza di Spagna

MONUMENTAL ROME,
P. 2, D2

Named after the residence of the Spanish ambassador
to the Vatican, the square and the famous Spanish Steps
are favorite gathering spots, especially for young people. Pietro Bernini's Barcaccia fountain stands at the
foot of the stairway. Next to the stairs is the Keats-
Shelley memorial, the house where Keats died (open
Monday through Friday 9 A.M. to 12:30 P.M. and 3:30
to 6 P.M., 2:30 to 5 P.M. in winter). The A line metro
stops just off the square.

Nearby: Piazza del Popolo; the Trevi Fountain; and
some great shopping.

Just before the square is the famous **Caffè Greco,** on
the left, which has always attracted artists and intellectu-
als. A brief closing by health authorities has not tainted its
reputation, though some cynics say the coffee is no longer
the same. Here one pays for the atmosphere and indifferent waiters in tails.

Piazza Navona

MONUMENTAL ROME,
P. 2, C3

This rectangular piazza is a baroque masterpiece, one
of the finest in Europe, dominated by Bernini's **Fountain of the Four Rivers.** His **Moor** and **Neptune**

Caravaggio, *Conversion of St. Paul* (1601–1602), Cerasi Chapel, Church of Santa Maria del Popolo

Unlike the patrons of the Renaissance, who valued stateliness and order above all, the public of the baroque period in the early 17th century thrilled to the drama of unruly passions. A fascination with religious mysticism swept Italy, as well as a taste for violent and theatrical subject matter in art. Caravaggio was well equipped by temperament to satisfy the craving. A notorious ruffian, he was forced to flee Rome in 1606 after murdering a rival at a tennis match.

His undisciplined genius is evident in the *Conversion of St. Paul.* This painting, hidden in a dark alcove of the church, is meant to bewilder. (A coin-activated lamp dimly illuminates the work.) St. Paul is shown at the moment of his conversion, overpowered by a religious vision that sweeps him from his horse as he travels the road to Damascus. Like the fallen rider, the viewer at first may feel somewhat disoriented. The low angle of vision draws the eye close to the ground, where St. Paul seems in danger of being trampled. The foreground is enlarged by the curtain of darkness behind it, and the combined effects of radical foreshortening, eerie light, crowding, and overlapping limbs contribute to an impression of claustrophobia; the transition in the saint's life is a violent one.

The painting's realism is unrelenting. Notice the furrowed brow and the varicose veins on the leg of the servant who is trying to control the horse. In an age of highly stylized baroque, Caravaggio insisted on the literal. His grubby exuberance shocked his contemporaries, but by the time he died at 38 (appropriately, of a fever), he was acknowledged as a master throughout Italy.

—Michael Hinden

fountains at opposite extremes of the piazza complete the spectacle. Facing the central Bernini fountain is the

Church of Sant'Agnese in Agone, with a baroque facade by Borromini. Bernini and Borromini were intense rivals, and local legend says Bernini purposefully fashioned the fountain's figures to recoil from the church. Borromini responded with an indignant Sant'Agnese atop the facade, whose turned head totally ignores the fountain below.

The Square has an active nightlife, with a number of caffès and great people-watching.

Nearby: The Pantheon.

Roman Forum

The Roman Forum lies in what was once a marshy valley between the sloping hills of Quirinale, Viminale, Palatine, and Capitoline. ("Forum" is derived from the Latin for "beyond inhabited areas.") The adjacent forums were constructed when this center became too small for meetings, judicial hearings, and sessions on public and commercial affairs. A detailed map of the ruins is essential to fully appreciate this heartland of Imperial Rome (open 9 A.M. to one hour before sunset, from 10 A.M. Sunday; closed Tuesday).

Among the more important ruins are the 179 B.C. **Basilica Emilia;** the **Curia** meeting place for senators; the **Tomb of Romulus** with the oldest known Latin inscription, "lapis niger"; the **Triumphal Arch of Septimus Severus** (A.D. 203); the A.D. 608 **Column of Phocas** (ruler of the Eastern Empire); and the **Via Sacra,** which led to a number of sanctuaries.

On the Via Sacra is the **Basilica Giulia** law courts next to the **Temple of Saturn.** Opposite the basilica are the remains of the **Temple of Caesar,** which was dedicated in 29 B.C. by Octavius on the spot where Caesar had been cremated.

The **Church of Santa Maria Antiqua** is the oldest Christian building in the forum (but closed at press time). Early frescoes are in the former imperial building. Back on the Via Sacra is the **House of the Vestal Virgins,** where the Vestals lived, completely cut off from the outside world. If the sacred flame in their circular **temple** ever went out it was interpreted as an omen of impending misfortune.

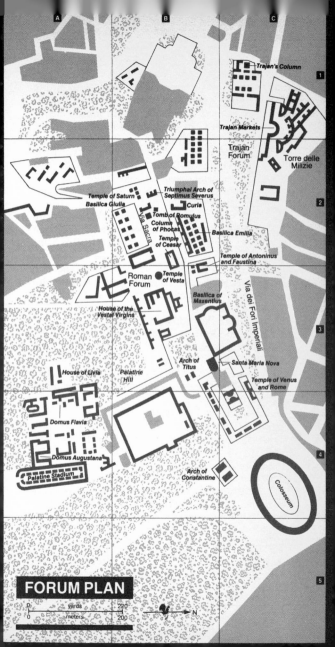

FORUM PLAN

Trajan's Column
Trajan Markets
Trajan Forum
Torre delle Milizie
Temple of Saturn
Basilica Giulia
Triumphal Arch of Septimus Severus
Curia
Tomb of Romulus
Via Sacra
Column of Phocas
Temple of Ceasar
Basilica Emilia
Temple of Antoninus and Faustina
Roman Forum
Temple of Vesta
House of the Vestal Virgins
Basilica of Maxentius
Via dei Fori Imperiali
House of Livia
Palatine Hill
Arch of Titus
Santa Maria Nova
Temple of Venus and Rome
Domus Flavia
Domus Augustana
Palatine Stadium
Arch of Constantine
Colosseum

0 yards 220
0 meters 200

N

Near the **Temple of Antoninus and Faustina** (A.D. 141) is the **cemetery** of the first Palatine inhabitants (ninth to sixth century B.C.). After the **Temple of the Diefied Romulus** (Tomb of Romulus), built by Maxentius after his son Romulus died in A.D. 309, is the fourth-century **Basilica of Maxentius,** where summer concerts are held.

These concerts are now the only evening activity in the Roman Forum. A "Sound and Light" show was evicted after several spectators were injured and irreparable damage to the ruins by both organizers and spectators was alleged.

Near the basilica is the church known both as **Santa Maria Nova** and **Santa Francesca Romana,** built in the second half of the tenth century to replace Santa Maria Antiqua. The 17th-century facade is by Carlo Lombardi. The Romanesque bell tower is of the 12th century. In the adjoining convent is the **Antiquarium Forense,** the Forum museum (open 9 A.M. to 6 P.M., to 3 P.M. in winter).

As you leave the church, to the right is the **Temple of Venus and Rome** begun by Hadrian, completed by Antoninus Pius, and rebuilt by Maxentius; and the **Arch of Titus** commemorating the victories of Vespasian and his son Titus over the Jews and the destruction of Jerusalem. Even today many visiting Jews refuse to pass under the arch.

In front of the Colosseum entrance to the Roman Forum, at the end of Via Sacra, is the **Arch of Constantine,** erected by the Senate and People of Rome (that's the meaning of *S.P.Q.R.,* which you'll see all over Rome, especially on manhole covers) in A.D. 315 to commemorate the emperor's victory over Maxentius at Ponte Milvio, a bridge that is still standing, between the former Olympic village and the Foro Italico athletic complex north of downtown Rome.

Take the B line metro to the Colosseo stop.
Nearby: The Colosseum and the Palatine Hill.

St. Peter's Square VATICAN, P. 1, A2

St. Peter's Basilica and its Bernini-framed piazza are the only parts of the independent Vatican state that are readily accessible free of charge to visitors. The independence of the Vatican was established by the first Lateran Pact, between Fascist Italy and the Holy See. The pact was altered recently, confirming many of the church's rights in the Italian state, but it was established by the government of then-Premier Bettino Craxi, a Socialist, that Catholicism was no longer to be considered the state religion.

The basilica that replaced the original one built by Emperor Constantine over St. Peter's tomb in A.D. 324 is the combination of efforts by Bramante, Michelangelo, Maderna, and Bernini. Of the five entrances into the world's largest church, (610 feet by 443 feet and 144 feet high), on the far right is the Holy Door, opened only during Holy Years. To the immediate right inside the basilica is Michelangelo's triumph in marble, the *Pietà.* It is now under protective glass and fully restored, after being damaged by a hammer-wielding Australian twenty years ago. Farther toward the front is the entrance to the dome; you can walk all the way up or travel part way by elevator, part way by stairs. It's a tiring trip, but the view makes the effort worthwhile.

The center altar is dominated by Bernini's half-styled, half-sculptured *baldacchino.* Only the pope celebrates mass from the high altar, which sits above the remains of St. Peter.

The left side of the Latin-cross church is the richest in sculpture, and features the **tombs of Innocent VIII, Leo XI de'Medici,** and **Alexander VII.** Entrance to the **Treasury** is to the left of the high altar, near the monument to Pius VIII.

In the apse in the front of the basilica is the **Throne of St. Peter** by Bernini, a great bronze work encasing a wooden chair said to have been St. Peter's; the throne floats on clouds toward the Holy Spirit in the stained-glass window above.

On the left of the basilica is the **Vatican information office,** tel. (06) 6982, where arrangements may be made for the two-hour tours (Lit. 9,000) of the **Vatican gardens** every morning except Wednesday and Sunday (when papal audiences and the papal benediction to the faithful gathered in the square are held if the

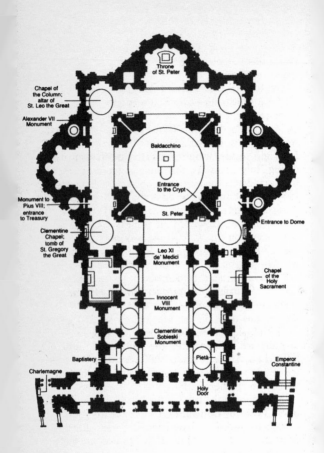

Throne of St. Peter

Chapel of the Column; altar of St. Leo the Great

Alexander VII Monument

Baldacchino

Entrance to the Crypt

St. Peter

Entrance to Dome

Monument to Pius VIII; entrance to Treasury

Clementine Chapel; tomb of St. Gregory the Great

Leo XI de' Medici Monument

Chapel of the Holy Sacrament

Innocent VIII Monument

Clementina Sobieski Monument

Baptistery

Pietà

Emperor Constantine

Charlemagne

Holy Door

ST. PETER'S

N

Pope is in Rome). The tours are limited to 33 persons; no reservations are taken by telephone.

Arrangements to visit the **catacombs** under St. Peter's may be made at the Ufficio Scavi, tel. (06) 6985318. You probably will have to wait, due to the great number of people who want to make this tour. Underground paths lead as far as the obelisk in the center of St. Peter's Square.

The **twin fountains** in the piazza were originally one; it was moved to make room for the obelisk and a replica of the fountain was constructed to balance the other side of the square.

Papal Audiences

Tickets for papal audiences, held on Wednesdays, should be sought through local dioceses before leaving home. There is often a last-minute possibility at the Vatican Prefecture (at the top of the stairs that begin under the colonnade on the right side of the basilica), where all uncollected tickets are returned and made available Tuesday on a first-come, first-served basis. Commercial tour companies also have tickets available to members of their coach tours. No tickets are needed for the Sunday blessing, held at noon, when the Pope appears at his apartment window in Rome or at the balcony of his summer house at Castel Gandolfo.

Take the A line metro to Ottaviano; the number 30 tram to Piazza Risorgimento; or the number 64 bus to the end of the line.
Nearby: The Vatican Museums and Castel Sant'Angelo.

San Giovanni in Laterano (St. John Lateran) and the Holy Stairs

ARCHAEOLOGICAL ROME, P. 7, F4

The cathedral of Rome, the cathedral of the Pope, stands in the piazza of the same name. The baptistery (open 8 A.M. to noon and 4 to 6 P.M.) is worth a visit for its eight mosaics of the life of John the Baptist. The Holy Stairs (8 A.M. to 12:30 P.M. and 3 to 7 P.M., from 3:30 P.M. May to September) are reputedly the original 28 marble stairs that Christ climbed in Pilate's palace in Jerusalem. The cathedral is just off the A line metro, at the beginning of the Via Appia Nuova.

San Pietro in Vincoli (St. Peter in Chains)

ARCHAEOLOGICAL ROME, P. 7, D3/E3

This fifth-century church houses the alleged chains of St. Peter and the beginning of the tomb commissioned by the megalomaniacal Pope Julius II of Michelangelo. The skyscraper proportions of the tomb, which was to be placed in St. Peter's, were never realized, but Michelangelo's overpowering Carrara marble statue of *Moses* is considered by many to be his greatest sculpture. Folklore has the master rapping his hammer against the work when completed and ordering, "Speak!"

Take the B line metro to Cavour.

Nearby: The Colosseum and Santa Maria Maggiore.

Santa Maria Maggiore

TERMINI, P. 3, E3

One of Rome's four major basilicas, this church was begun in the fifth century. Of special interest are the baroque Chapel of Sixtus V and Pauline Chapel. The campanile is the highest in Rome. The church stands in the Piazza Santa Maria Maggiore, just off the B metro line, near the Termini stop.

Nearby: The church of Santa Maria degli Angeli; the Diocletian Baths; and the National Museum of Rome.

Trevi Fountain

MONUMENTAL ROME, P. 2, D2

Rome's most famous fountain was built in the 18th century. The central figure of Neptune appears to call for calm. The City shows up promptly every evening to remove the coins tossed in by tourists, which had caused rivalry between juvenile gangs after the money. Turned off in the evening, the fountain invites contemplation in spite of the masses of tourists. On the square are a number of shoe stores catering to the bargain-conscious.

Take the A line metro; the Barberini or Spagna stops are the closest.

Nearby: The Piazza di Spagna and the Pantheon.

✦ For daytime or evening refreshment at number 90 is **Claudio Patassini's** bar, with a wide assortment of ice cream and fruit drinks to beat the summer heat, and an excellent hot chocolate to accompany an equally large number of pastries in cooler weather.

Vatican Museums

VATICAN, P. 1, A2

The most famous section of these museums, which house an enormous collection of works, is the Sistine Chapel. Right before you enter the chapel are the Raphael Rooms, painted by Raphael for Pope Julius II while Michelangelo was working on the Sistine ceiling. (Michelangelo's *Last Judgment* on the Sistine wall was painted more than twenty years after he completed work on the ceiling.) The Vatican Museums are open 9 A.M. to 2 P.M. Monday through Saturday, and the last Sunday of the month (when they're free). During July, August, September and at Easter, hours extend to 5 P.M. Take the A line metro, the number 30 tram, or the number 64 bus, all to the end of the line.

Nearby: St. Peter's Square and Basilica; Castel Sant'Angelo.

Michelangelo, *The Sistine Chapel Ceiling* (1508–1512)

"I'm no painter," Michelangelo protested, trying to fob off the job on Raphael. But Pope Julius II prevailed, and in 1508, the renowned sculptor mounted scaffolding to begin the most ambitious artistic undertaking of the Renaissance. Always impatient, Michelangelo fired his assistants early on. Four years later, after back-wrenching toil in contorted positions, he was finished. Michelangelo's frescoes cover nearly 6,000 square feet of a difficult vaulted surface and include hundreds of figures: Old Testament prophets, sibyls, and various supporting characters for the great biblical epic from *Genesis* that spans the central vault.

The ceiling is crowded with drama. Picture the nine central panels as a tragedy in three acts, each divided into three scenes. Act I, shrouded in mystery, hints at the Creation: In the beginning, God separates light from darkness, creates the heavens, and separates the waters from the land. Act II begins in hope and ends in despair: the Creation of Adam and Eve, and the Temptation and Expulsion from the Garden. Act III depicts the Flood: Noah's Sacrifice, the

Deluge, and Noah's Drunkenness. The scenes were painted in reverse narrative order; Michelangelo began with Noah's sin, and then inched his way across the ceiling toward that moment of visionary creation when the universe first sprang into being at God's command.

In all of Western art, there is no more famous image than the central panel, where an all-powerful Creator, with flowing robe and beard, extends his hand to Adam, linking the human and the Divine. Pictured before the Fall, Adam, godlike himself, truly is formed in his maker's image. Waiting to receive the spark of life, he is separated from perfection by a fingertip only.

—Michael Hinden

Michelangelo, *The Last Judgment* (1535–1541)

The far wall of the Sistine Chapel boasts a masterpiece every bit as impressive as the ceiling frescoes, but this awe-inspiring *Last Judgment* was painted more than twenty years later. The Rome that Michelangelo knew had now was split in two; in 1527 Charles V's invading army had stabled its horses in the Sistine Chapel. In response, the Counter-Reformation was underway, battering the Renaissance ideal of humanism.

In executing the *Last Judgment,* Michelangelo gave vent to his dismay, adding a terrifying final act to the drama of human destiny depicted on the ceiling. Angels summon the dead with trumpet blasts; corpses and skeletons rise from the grave; the righteous (on the left) ascend, while the wicked (on the right) are cast down. At the center, a beardless, powerful Christ threatens evildoers with an upraised arm, while Charon waits below to ferry the damned.

Michelangelo spent four years laboring on the Sistine ceiling. The *Last Judgment* cost him six more. Toward the end, the artist drew his own self-portrait on the flayed skin dangling from the hand of martyred St. Bartholomew, who sits at Christ's left knee. By painting his facial signature on this grisly trophy, Michelangelo may have been expressing his anguish at the world's injustice—and his own spiritual exhaustion.

—Michael Hinden

Raphael, *The School at Athens*
(1508–1511)

Balance, harmony, and grace are the characteristics of Raphael's style, but the tensions that are brought under control in this sweeping narrative of ancient philosophy must have tested his unifying powers. In *The School at Athens,* formal balance mirrors the reconciliation of philosophical opposites.

At the center of the painting, Plato and Aristotle resume their age-old quarrel. Plato gestures upward, asserting the realm of Pure Ideas; Aristotle extends a downward palm, claiming the domain of Nature. Between them, they divide ancient philosophy into two camps. On Plato's side are the metaphysicians such as Pythagoras (in the foreground), shown working on his harmonic tablets, while Aristotle gathers on his side the scientists and mathematicians, such as Euclid, drawing with his compass.

It has been suggested, considering the fresco's placement in the heart of the papal court, that the painting may have been intended to convey a timely message to Raphael's contemporaries: If science and metaphysics are reconcilable, then might not the entire tradition of pagan philosophy be reconciled with the Church? Such was the hope of the Renaissance humanists, and Raphael had enlisted in their cause.

As his model for Plato, Raphael chose Leonardo da Vinci. The young artist himself (wearing a black cap) peers out of the painting at the far right. Michelangelo inspired the dejected figure in the foreground, hunched on the steps, head in hand. Only Michelangelo appears unmollified, unable to resolve his lifelong struggle to synthesize pagan and Christian teachings.

Symbolically, the majestic vault encompasses them all, repeating its design in a series of distant arches and hemispheres of sky, suggesting an endless progression of visual and philosophical horizons.

—Michael Hinden

Villa Borghese

Created by Cardinal Scipione Borghese in the 17th century, this park, three and a half miles square, makes a pleasant break from city streets. On the grounds are the Borghese Museum and Gallery, Piazza Scipione Borghese 3; telephone (06) 858577, featuring works of Italian masters; the Modern Art Gallery, Viale delle Belle Arti 131; telephone (06) 802751; and the Renaissance Villa Giulia, now the National Etruscan Museum, Piazzale di Villa Giulia 9, off the Viale delle Belle Arti; take tram number 30. All three are open 9 A.M. to 2 P.M. Tuesday through Saturday, to 1 P.M. Sunday; closed Monday. Villa Giulia is also open Wednesday afternoons. Bus number 490 passes through the park.

Excursions into rural Lazio, including Tivoli, are discussed later in this chapter.

Museum Hours

Unless otherwise specified, museums usually are open from 9 A.M. to 2 P.M. Tuesday through Saturday, to 1 P.M. on Sunday and holidays. You cannot enter during the last hour; some more abrupt ticket takers close even earlier.

Though afternoon and evening hours are sometimes given, sites often are not actually open. Check before making special trips: Telephone the gallery or museum directly to confirm the hours.

5

TOURING

Since a normal lifetime does not offer the opportunity to properly visit all that both Rome and the Vatican have to offer, organized tours merit special consideration here. As always, tours mean running with the herd, but they provide a reasonable means of visiting the most in the least amount of time.

There are a number of reputable tour operators in Rome. Each has its share of arrangements with hotels ranging from luxury to economy class. Some will make pickup arrangements, others require that clients reach a central meeting point.

Practically all hotels have arrangements with a tour company; the desk will provide brochures upon request, collect payment, and provide tickets for excursions.

The city is basically divided into four half-day excursions by all companies. There may be variations from the following facsimile, but they will be minor. The companies are in competition, but also in close collaboration, especially on out-of-Rome excursions when they often pool clients to fill tours on the less popular longer trips.

One morning excursion stops at the Trevi Fountain, St. Peter's Basilica, and the Janiculum (the balcony of Rome behind Trastevere, offering extensive views over the city). Sites explained by an English-speaking guide en route include: Via Veneto, Palazzo Margherita (now the U.S. Embassy), the Quirinale Palace residence of the Italian president, Piazza Venezia (with the monument to Vittorio Emanuele and Mussolini's balcony), Teatro di Marcello, the Vesta and Fortuna Virile temples, Bocca della Verità (in the Santa Maria in Cosmedin Church), Tiberina Island, the medieval Jewish quarter and temple, Trastevere, and the papal fortress of Castel Sant'Angelo.

Another morning tour is dedicated to the Vatican Museums, with emphasis on the Raphael Rooms and the Sistine Chapel. Also visited in the museums are the candelabra, tapestry, and map galleries.

There are two afternoon city tours. One stops in Piazza Venezia, the Capitoline Hill (Rome's city hall on Piazza del Campidoglio, the square designed by Michelangelo, offering a view over the Roman Forum and the Colosseum), St Paul's Outside the Walls (one of the four cathedrals in Rome), and the church of San Pietro in Vincoli (with the statue of Moses by Michelangelo). The tour passes the Palatine Hill, the former Circus Maximus, and the Pyramid of Caius Cestius.

The other afternoon tour visits the basilicas of Santa Maria Maggiore; San Giovanni in Laterano, with the alleged Holy Stairs that Christ climbed at Pontius Pilate's palace; and one of the major catacombs on the Appian Way. The tour drives by the Triton fountain at Piazza Barberini, the tomb of Cecilia Metella, and the Baths of Caracalla, where summer open-air opera is staged.

The only tour that sweeps through the entire city is the night excursion that stops only at the Trevi Fountain and Piazza Navona. This is a good, economical orientation taking in many of the major sights. This tour comes in three versions: a simple tour; Rome by night with either a spaghetti or pizza stop afterwards; or a Tour plus a visit to the Fantasie di Trastevere restaurant for dinner and a folk show featuring Roman songs in the former Tiberine Theater.

Half-day excursions out of the city take in Tivoli, the ancient Roman seaport of Ostia, and the Albani Hills, which include the summer papal residence at Castel Gandolfo.

Most tour companies will arrange for a papal audience either in Rome or Castel Gandolfo. There are a number of combination tours to Capri, Pompeii, Sorrento, and Amalfi. One-day tours go to Florence, Assisi, Anzio, and Nettuno (to visit the U.S. war cemetery), as well as an Etruscan tour that is one of the best of the lot.

Leading agencies are:

American Express, Piazza di Spagna 35; tel. (06) 6796108. Appian Line, Via Barberini 109; tel. (06) 464151. CIT, Piazza della Repubblica 68; tel. (06) 47941. Carrani, Via V.E. Orlando 95; tel. (06) 4742501. Green Line, Via Farini 5a; tel. (06) 4744857. Vastours, Via Piemonte 34; tel. (06) 4814309.

A Tour of Michelangelo's Rome

In 1505, Michelangelo was summoned from Florence to Rome by Pope Julius II. With his departure, the center of gravity of the Italian Renaissance shifted south. Michelangelo's Roman commissions transformed some of the city's most important landmarks.

Begin in the morning with a visit to Vatican City, starting in **St. Peter's Square (Piazza San Pietro).** Michelangelo adapted plans by Bramante in designing the present **basilica** soon after his arrival. Later architects significantly altered his cohesive design, but the colossal dome, surely the most beautiful in Europe, retains his lofty vision. It was not built until after Michelangelo's death.

Entering the huge basilica, locate the *Pietà* in the first chapel to the right. Carved in 1499 when the sculptor was only 24 years old, this was Michelangelo's first masterpiece, and it gained him immediate fame. Its poignancy and beauty of expression are unrivaled. Visitors praise the anatomical accuracy of the figures, but in fact Mary is larger than Christ and paradoxically younger. Through these subtle reversals, Michelangelo stresses the Virgin's eternal youth and at the same time her motherly embrace of her martyred son.

Devote the remainder of the morning and early afternoon to the **Vatican Museums,** which include the Sistine Chapel. The various rooms are open from 9 A.M. to 2 P.M., to 5 P.M. in July, August, and September; closed Sunday. Choose one of the self-guided tours depending on the amount of time at your disposal, and follow the colored arrows. Highlights of a Michelangelo tour might include the *Laocoön Group* in the Octagonal Court and the *Apollo Belvedere* in an adjacent room, two masterpieces of sculpture from antiquity that Michelangelo admired. The **Sistine Chapel** itself is overpowering and simply cannot be absorbed by just walking through. Bring opera glasses or binoculars and plan to linger.

After a late lunch, visit Michelangelo's modification of Roman civic architecture on the **Capitoline Hill** (the **Campidoglio**). Both the **Piazza del Campidoglio** and the **Palazzo Nuovo** were built to Michelangelo's specifications.

Conclude the tour with a visit to the Church of **(San Pietro in Vincoli) (St. Peter in Chains),** in the vicinity of the Colosseum. Michelangelo's majestic *Moses* (1515) is here, although it was originally designed for Pope Julius's unfinished tomb. This wrathful, muscular giant appears about to rise from his seat, transported with fury at those who have rejected God's laws. Along with *David* and the *Pietà*, the *Moses* is one of Michelangelo's supreme achievements in sculpture.

In this connection I wish to say one word about Michelangelo Buonarroti. I used to worship the mighty genius of Michelangelo—that man who was great in poetry, painting, sculpture, architecture—great in everything he undertook. But I do not want Michelangelo for breakfast—for luncheon—for dinner—for tea—for supper—for between meals. I like a change occasionally. In Genoa he designed everything; in Milan he or his pupils designed everything; he designed the Lake of Como; in Padua, Verona, Venice, Bologna, who did we ever hear of from guides but Michelangelo? In Florence he painted everything, designed everything nearly, and what he did not design he used to sit on a favorite stone and look at, and they showed us the stone. In Pisa he designed everything but the old shot tower, and they would have attributed that to him if it had not been so awfully out of the perpendicular. He designed the piers of Leghorn and the custom-house regulations of Civitavecchia. But here—here it is frightful. He designed St. Peter's; he designed the Pope; he designed the Pantheon, the uniform of the Pope's soldiers, the Tiber, the Vatican, the Coliseum, the Capitol, the Tarpeian Rock, the Barberini Palace, St. John Lateran, the Campagna, the Appian Way, the Seven Hills, the Baths of Caracalla, the Claudian Aqueduct, the Cloaca Maxima—the eternal bore designed the Eternal City, and unless all men and books do lie, he painted everything in it! Dan said the other day to the guide, "Enough, enough, enough! Say no more! Lump the whole thing! Say that the Creator made Italy from designs by Michelangelo!"

I never felt so fervently thankful, so soothed, so tranquil, so filled with a blessed peace as I did yesterday when I learned that Michelangelo was dead.

—Mark Twain
The Innocents Abroad, 1869

6

CITY LISTINGS

CHURCHES

All sights are keyed into the page number of the color
Rome map (in the back of the book) and the map coordinates at which they appear.

Chiesa Nuova (New Church)   **MONUMENTAL ROME, P. 2, B3**

See Santa Maria in Vallicella.

San Carlo alle Quattro Fontane (San Carlino)

     MONUMENTAL ROME, P. 3, D2

Via Quirinale and Via Quattro Fontane.
Familiarly known as San Carlino, this oval church was designed by
Francesco Borromini and houses one of the four fountains built by
Pope Sixtus V.

San Clemente   **ARCHAEOLOGICAL ROME, P. 7, E4**

Via di San Giovanni in Laterano, behind the Colosseum. Mon.–Sat.
9–11:30 A.M., 3:30–6:30 P.M., Sun. 10–11:30 A.M., 3:30–6:30 P.M.
On the lower level of this ancient site (various levels of ancient Rome
are exposed as you descend) is a fourth-century church dedicated
to St. Clement and cared for by Irish Domenicans. A splendid mosaic
depicting *The Triumph of the Cross* can be seen in the apse of the
upper church.

San Giovanni in Laterano   **ARCHAEOLOGICAL ROME, P. 7, F4**

Piazza di San Giovanni in Laterano, near beginning of Via Appia
Nuova; Baptistery: 8 A.M.–noon, 4–6 P.M.; Holy Stairs: 6 A.M.–12:30
P.M.; May–Sept. from 3:30 P.M. only.
See Priorities.

Francesco Borromini, San Carlo alle Quattro Fontane, (1633–1683)

Some have called the passion and drama of this church wanton and immoral. Before receiving the commission for San Carlo, Borromini apprenticed with his uncle, the architect Maderna, on the completion of St. Peter's. For San Carlo Borromini rejected Maderna's use of clear, geometric forms, favoring ovals and polygons, which resulted in a new dynamism. The design is a case of a master in control of his powers, working with a modest commission and a restricted urban site to produce a brillant tour de force.

San Carlino (as it is familiarly known) is imbedded in baroque Rome. The church incorporates one of the four fountains built by Pope Sixtus V as part of his plan to mark significant places and call attention to important views.

Movement is the major issue in Borromini's church. The facade displays compressed and distorted forms combined with sinuous, undulating lines. The campanile and cupola bulge out at the corner, making the front shrug its "shoulders."

The interior of the church arouses both awe and anxiety. As with the facade, tension is created by classical forms thrusting here and pulling there, stretching and compressing the idea of the centrally aligned church. The dome is articulated with coffers in the shapes of crosses, hexagons, and octagons, exaggerating its depth. The columns seem to offer tenuous support in the face of all this activity.

—Mary Beth Betts and Charles Ayes

San Paolo Fuori le Mura (St. Peter's Beyond the Walls)

OUTSKIRTS

Via Ostiense; cloisters open 9 A.M.–1 P.M., 3–6 P.M.
The basilica is a shrine to the martyred St. Paul and remains a required stop for Holy Year Pilgrims. The original fourth-century church was destroyed by fire in 1823 and has been rebuilt in the early Christian style; it contains masterpieces salvaged from the blaze.

San Pietro in Vincoli (St. Peter in Chains)

ARCHAEOLOGICAL ROME, P. 7, D3/E3

Piazza San Pietro in Vincoli off Via Cavour
See Priorities.

San Prassede

TERMINI, P. 3, E3

Via San Martino ai Monti

The most important Byzantine monument in Rome. The Flagellation Column in the church was brought to Rome in 1223, and is believed to be the column to which Christ was tied and whipped in Jerusalem.

Sant' Agnese in Agone
MONUMENTAL ROME, P. 2, C3

Piazza Navona
This church features a baroque facade by Borromini and faces one of Bernini's fountains in Piazza Navona. Bernini and Borromini were rivals and local legend says that Bernini purposely fashioned the fountain's figures to recoil from the church. In response, Borromini positioned Sant' Agnese atop the facade with her head turned to ignore the fountain below.

Santa Maria d' Aracoeli
MONUMENTAL ROME, P. 6, D4

Piazza del Campidoglio
Frescoes by Pinturicchio decorate a chapel in this church which was built on the site of an ancient fortress and the Temple of Juno.

Santa Maria degli Angeli
TERMINI, P. 3, E2

Piazza della Repubblica
Michelangelo transformed part of the fourth-century Diocletian Baths into this church on commission from Pius IV. However, much of the church was redesigned in Baroque style in the 1700s.

Santa Maria dei Miracoli
MONUMENTAL ROME, P. 2, C1

Via del Corso, Piazza del Popolo
This church and its twin, Santa Maria di Monte Santi, frame the central Via del Corso. Both are Baroque, and are the work of Rainaldi, Bernini, and Carlo Fontana.

Santa Maria del Popolo
MONUMENTAL ROME, P. 2, C1

Piazza del Popolo
The first chapel of this church houses frescoes by Pinturicchio and two masterpieces by Caravaggio, among other treasures. See Piazza del Popolo in Priorities.

Santa Maria della Vittoria
TERMINI, P. 3, E2

Via XX Settembre
A Baroque church most notable for Bernini's *St. Teresa in Ecstasy*, in the Coronaro Chapel, a masterpiece which combines sculpture, architecture, metallurgy, painting, and theatrical design.

Santa Maria di Monte Santi
MONUMENTAL ROME, P. 2, C1

Via del Corso, Piazza del Popolo
See Santa Maria dei Miracoli.

Santa Maria in Cosmedin
ARCHAEOLOGICAL ROME, P. 6, D4

Piazza Bocca della Verita
A beautiful sixth-century medieval church featuring a seven story bell tower. Outside the church is the Bocca della Verita (Mouth of Truth),

Gianlorenzo Bernini, *St. Teresa in Ecstasy* (1645-52)

In the 17th century, while Protestant churches were being stripped of decoration, the spirit of the Counter-Reformation came alive in Rome, fighting to win back the soul of Europe through prodigious works of art. In Bernini, the movement found a sculptor whose talent was said to rival Michelangelo's.

More than an exquisite statue—although it certainly is that—*St. Teresa* in Santa Maria della Vittoria orchestrates a multimedia environment, combining sculpture (the central figures carved in gleaming marble), architecture (the opulent canopy above), metallurgy (the heavenly rays of gilded bronze), painting (the chapel's ornate ceiling), and theatrical design (the ensemble as a whole). The work might be thought of as a grandiloquent opera without sound.

The story of St. Teresa of Avila was known to everyone. A Spanish mystic of the 16th century, she recorded in her *Autobiography* a series of strange visitations by an angel who repeatedly plunged a dart into her bosom, causing her to swoon in delicious pain. To Teresa, this was the arrow of Divine love. Of course, there have been Freudian explanations of Teresa's fainting spells. Bernini himself seems well aware of the erotic parallels in his treatment of the subject. The saint's parted lips, curled toes, and posture of abandon suggest that the sculptor based his interpretation of mystical transport on his knowledge of sexual response. Baroque artists often thought of physical and spiritual rapture as mutually enlightening. Bernini was devout, and the religiosity of the ensemble is indisputable, as is his astonishing skill in three-dimensional representation.

Bernini's stamp as an architect is visible all over Rome, in the city's fountains, buildings, and piazzas, and most noticeably St. Peter's Square.

—Michael Hinden

once used as a drain cover. Legend claimed that anyone putting a hand in the drain, sculpted as a face, would lose it if telling a lie.

Santa Maria in Trastevere **TRASTEVERE, P. 6, C4**
Off via della Lungaretto, in Piazza Santa Maria in Trastevere

The exact origin of the church (third or fourth-century) is uncertain, but the present basilica was built in the twelfth century, and renovated several times. Of particular interest are the twelfth-to-thirteenth-century mosaics on the facade, and the ornate wood ceiling. Once a month, in front of the church, a group of Sicilian doctors distribute, free of charge, a cancer drug that the Italian authorities refuse to legalize; under the Lateran Pacts, the Vatican has extraterritorial rights over the church property, and the doctors are protected.

Santa Maria in Vallicella (Chiesa Nuova)

MONUMENTAL ROME, P. 2, B3

Up Corso Vittorio Emanuele, near Palazzo della Cancelleria
This 16th-century church contains a fine high altarpiece and two paintings by Rubens.

Santa Maria Maggiore

TERMINI, P. 3, E3

Between Piazza dell'Esquilino and Piazza Santa Maria Maggiore
See Priorities.

Santa Maria sopra Minerva

MONUMENTAL ROME, P. 2, C3

Piazza della Minerva (near the Pantheon)
Founded in the eighth century on the remains of a temple to Minerva, this church was rebuilt in Gothic style in the 12th century and houses a number of impressive works. The facade was rebuilt during the Renaissance.

Sistine Chapel

VATICAN, P. 1, A1

See Vatican Museums.

St. Peter's Basilica

VATICAN, P. 1, A2

St. Peter's Square
See Priorities.

HISTORICAL SIGHTS

Arc Pacis Augustae

MONUMENTAL ROME, P. 2, C2

On the banks of the Tiber, near the Piazza Augustus Imperatore.
Open usual hours, plus Tues., Thurs., Sat., 4:30–8 P.M., April–Oct.
A reconstruction of a monumental altar built by order of the Roman Senate to honor Augustus and the peace that folowed his victories in Spain and Gaul.

Arch of Constantine

ARCHAEOLOGICAL ROME, P. 7, D4

In front of Colosseum, at the entrance to Via Sacra
This monument was erected by the Senate and People of Rome in 315 to commemorate Constantine's victory over Maxentius at Ponte Milvio.

Area Sacra of Largo di Torre Argentino

MONUMENTAL ROME, P. 6, D3

Corso Vittorio Emanuele, Piazza Venezia
Imperial ruins which were once the site of four Republican temples; these are earliest ancient remains in central Rome.

Barcaccia Fountain

MONUMENTAL ROME, P. 2, D2

Piazza di Spagna
A perfect setting for people watching, this fountain was believed to have been designed by Pietro Bernini, the father of the more famous Gianlorenzo. See Piazza di Spagna in Priorities.

Baths of Caracalla

ARCHAEOLOGICAL ROME, P. 7, D5

Viale delle Terme di Caracalla; Tues.–Sat. 9 A.M.–6 P.M., Sun. and Mon. to 1 P.M.; for opera information, tel. (06) 5758300
See Priorities.

Bernini's Fountain of Four Rivers

MONUMENTAL ROME, P. 2, C3

Piazza Navona
Commissioned by Innocent X, this is probably Bernini's most famous fountain. The figures are said to represent the four rivers of the Nile, Ganges, Danube, and Plate. The fountain faces the church of Sant' Agnese by Borromini, Bernini's rival, and stories claimed that Bernini fashioned the fountain's figures to recoil from the church.

Capitol (Campidoglio)

MONUMENTAL ROME, P. 6, D3

Piazza del Campidoglio
See Priorities.

Castel Sant' Angelo

VATICAN, PP. 1/2, B2

Lungotevere Castello
See Priorities.

Catacombs

ARCHAEOLOGICAL ROME

San Callisto, Appian Way 110; San Sebastiano, Appian Way 136; 8:30 A.M.–noon; 2:30–5:30 P.M. in summer, in winter, to 5 P.M.
See Priorities.

Circus Maximus

ARCHAEOLOGICAL ROME, P. 6, D4

At the foot of the Palatine Hill
Located northwest of the Baths of Caracalla is a rectangular field that was once the Circus Maximus. Now stripped of all artifacts, the area had been used for chariot races, housing hundreds of thousands of spectators. It is sometimes used for summer film shows and cultural events and is now considered public ground.

Colosseum ARCHAEOLOGICAL ROME, P. 7, D4
Via dei Fori Imperiali; 9 A.M.–3:30 P.M. in winter, to 7 P.M. in summer, Sun. to 1 P.M.
See Priorities.

Diocletian Baths

Piazza della Repubblica

The remains of the largest of all bath complexes is located in Piazza della Repubblica. Michelangelo transformed part of the baths into the church of Santa Maria degli Angeli, but you can still get a sense of their vast size and layout.

Mausoleum of Augustus

Piazza Augustus Imperatore

This imposing brick mausoleum was previously used as a fortress, a circus and concert hall, and an amphitheater before extensive archaeological excavations, which ended in 1936. The mausoleum is now closed to the public.

Moor Fountain

Piazza Navona

This Baroque fountain features a Moor grasping a dolphin and is complemented by the Neptune Fountain at the opposite end of the piazza. See Piazza Navona under Priorities.

Neptune Fountain

Piazza Navona

This fountain wasn't completed until the late 1800s and faces the Moor Fountain. Again, see Piazza Navona under Priorities.

Palatine Hill

9 A.M.–7 P.M., winters to 5 P.M.
See Priorities.

Palazzo del Quirinale

Quirinale Hill; tel (06) 46991; open by appt. only.

This former royal palace is now the official residence of the president of Italy. The obelisk inside originally stood at the entrance to the mausoleum of Augustus, and was moved to its present location in 1587 by Pope Sixtus V. The gardens inside the palace are a beautiful oasis of green and silence in the center of this vibrant city.

Palazzo della Cancelleria

Corso Vittorio Emanuele

One of the finest Renaissance buildings in Rome, built for a nephew of Sixtus V, between 1485 and 1513.

Palazzo Farnese

Between Campo dei Fiore and the Tiber

This beautiful Renaissance building is now the French Embassy. Sangallo the Younger and Michelangelo contributed to the design of the palazzo, which contains a number of frescoes by Raphael. The building itself is closed to tourists.

Palazzo Venezia

One of the earliest Renaissance palaces in Rome, this became the seat of the Fascist Movement in Italy. From its first-floor balcony,

Mussolini announced Italy's ill-fated venture into World War II. One floor of the palace houses an art collection open to the public.

Pantheon MONUMENTAL ROME, P. 2, C3
Piazza della Rotonda
See Priorities.

Piazza del Campidoglio MONUMENTAL ROME, P. 6, D3

Capitoline Hill
This beautiful palace complex on Capitoline Hill was designed by Michelangelo. The equestrian statue of Marcus Aurelius was once in the center of the square, but has been removed and is undergoing renovation. See Capitol (Campidoglio) under Priorities.

Piazza Navona MONUMENTAL ROME, P. 2, C3
See Priorities.

Piazza del Popolo MONUMENTAL ROME, P. 2, C1
See Priorities.

Piazza di Spagna MONUMENTAL ROME, P. 2, D2
See Priorities.

Porto del Popolo MONUMENTAL ROME, P. 2, C1
Piazza del Popolo
This 17th-century facade is the entrance to monumental Rome at Piazza del Popolo and was designed by Bernini.

Roman Forum ARCHAEOLOGICAL ROME, PP. 6/7, D3/D4

9 A.M.–one hour before sunset; from 10 A.M. Sun., closed Tues.
See Priorities.

Trajan Forum ARCHAEOLOGICAL ROME, P. 2, D3
Via Magnanapoli off Via IV Novembre; 9 A.M.–1 P.M., 3–6 P.M.; mornings only on Sun; Oct. 1–May 31, 10 A.M.–4 P.M., closed Sun. and holidays. The most recent of the Imperial Forums, the Trajan Forum contains one of the most remarkable surviving monuments of ancient Rome, Trajan's column; spiriling bas-reliefs illustrate scenes of war against the Dacians. Next door are the Trajan Markets, which once contained shops.

Trevi Fountain MONUMENTAL ROME, P. 2, D2
Off Via del Tritone
See Priorities.

Walls of ancient Rome OUTSKIRTS
The walls extend around a good portion of the city. They begin at Porta del Popolo and run parallel to Viale del Muro Torto up to Porta Pinciana (at the top of the Via Veneto), then along Corso d'Italia to Porta Salaria, and around the Pretorian Camp as far as Porta Tiburtina and Porta San Lorenzo; then comes the stretch that is most evocative of their original defensive purpose—from Porta Latina to Porta San Sebastiano, which opens onto the Appian Way. Open to visitors at Via di Porta San Sebastiano 18, Tues.–Sat. 9 A.M.–1:50 P.M., Sun. and holidays 9 A.M.–1 P.M., Tues., Thurs. in summer, 4–7 P.M., closed Mon.

MUSEUMS

Borghese Museum and Gallery
BORGHESE, P. 3, D1

Piazza Scipione Borghese 3; tel. (06) 858577; Tues.–Sat. 9 A.M.–2 P.M., Sun. to 1 P.M., closed Mon.

This museum which features sculpture by Bernini and paintings by 16th-and 17th-century Italian masters, has been undergoing extensive renovation and may have limited access. Some of its major works are consequently being displayed elsewhere in the city, so please telephone the museum directly to obtain specific information.

Capitoline Museums (Palazzo Nuovo and Palazzo dei Conservatori)
MONUMENTAL ROME, P. 6, D3

Piazza del Campidoglio; tel. (06) 6782862; Tues.–Fri. 9 A.M.–2 P.M., Tues. and Thurs. also 5–8 P.M., Sat. to 11:30 P.M., Sun. to 1 P.M., closed Mon.

See Capitol in Priorities.

Galleria Colonna
MONUMENTAL ROME, P. 2, D3

Via della Pilotta 17; tel. (06) 6794362; open Sat. only, closed in Aug.

Facing the Piazza Santi Apostoli, this 17th-century gallery contains works by Van Dyck, Tintoretto, Veronese, and Annibale Caracci, among others.

Keats-Shelley Memorial
MONUMENTAL ROME, P. 2, D2

Piazza di Spagna; tel. (06) 6784235; Mon.–Fri. 9 A.M.–12:30 P.M., 3:30–6 P.M., winter 2:30–5 P.M., closed Sat., Sun.

Beside the Spanish Steps is the house where Keats died, which now houses a collection of memorabilia for students of Shelley and Keats.

Modern Art Gallery
BORGHESE, P. 2, D1

Viale delle Belle Arti 131; tel. (06) 802751; Tues.–Sat. 9 A.M.–2 P.M., Sun. to 1 P.M., closed Mon.

Located on the outer rim of Villa Borghese, the gallery stages special exhibits year-round to accompany permanent exhibits of Italian Impressionists, as well as futurist Umberto Boccioni and the metaphysical Giorgio De Chirico.

National Museum of Rome
TERMINI, P. 3, E2

Piazza della Republicca; 9 A.M.–1:45 P.M., Sun. to noon, closed Mon.

The museum has one of the largest collections of relics from ancient Rome.

Vatican Museums (including the **Sistine Chapel**)
VATICAN, P. 1, A2

Viale Vaticano; Mon.–Sat. 9 A.M.–2 P.M., to 5 P.M. during July, Aug., Easter, closed Sun. except the last Sun. in the month.

See Priorities.

Villa Giulia (Etruscan Museum) BORGHESE, P. 2, C1

Piazzale di Villa Giulia 9; tel. (06) 3601951. Tues.–Sat 9 A.M.–2 P.M., Wed. to 6:30 P.M. in winter, 3–7:30 in summer; Sun. to 1 P.M., closed Mon.

This 16th-century Rennaissance villa was built for Pope Julius III. Now it houses the National Etruscan Museum featuring artifacts from digs at Cerveteri and Veio, and an impressive collection of Etruscan art from the mysterious civilization who profoundly influenced Roman culture.

PARKS AND GARDENS

Villa Borghese BORGHESE, PP. 2–3, D1
See Priorities.

Etruscans

The Etruscans were the most important inhabitants of Italy prior to the Romans. From the eighth century B.C. to the third century B.C., when they were finally conquered their military and cultural superiority over the Italian tribes allowed them to dominate almost a third of Italy, including present day Tuscany, Umbria, and parts of Campania.

The Etruscan states were never a unified nation; rather, there were three main concentrations—Etruria, Campania, and the Po Valley—each with twelve capital cities. Among the cities ruled by the Etruscans were Perugia and Bologna in the north, Tarquinia and Caere (Cerveteri) in the environs of Rome, and Pompeii in the south. Historical evidence indicates that these cities felt no alliance with one another and were often engaged in civil wars. This, in addition to a series of invasions by the Gauls in the north and the Romans in the south, led to their decline. Today, for a number of reasons, little is known about the Etruscans; the only historical records of them come from their Roman conquerers who absorbed their civilization. Most information about Etruscan society comes from the burial rite.

Throughout Etruria the typical burial rite was cremation. The Etruscans believed that death was a journey rather than an end and treated their tombs as shrines for the dead. Many tombs were decorated with frescoes of daily life, jewelry, vases, and terracottas. While many of the tombs were looted or destroyed during excavations, you can still visit a few and the artifacts from many others have been preserved in Italy's museums. Among the "Etruscan places" worth visiting are Tarquinia, for the Museo Nazionale Etrusco and the Necropolis of Tarquinia where frescoes date from the 6C BC to the 2C BC, representing all phases of tomb painting, Perugia, for the Museo Archeologico Nazionale dell' Umbria and the Ipogeo dei Volumni, one of the finest Etruscan tombs dating from the 2C BC, and Cerveteri, the Etruscan city of Caere, for the Necropolis of the Banditaccia. Italy's largest and best collection of Etruscan artifacts is in the Villa Giulia in Rome.

—Charlotte Savidge

7

SHOPPING

Complaining about prices in Rome shops is as much a national as an international pastime. For the foreign traveler, the scales can tip noticeably according to the whims of the international exchange rate. For Italians, prices can roller-coaster from inventory time to the legitimate *saldi* (sales), at the end of the winter and summer seasons in particular. The between-season offerings in late spring and late fall often don't amount to much.

Sales generally begin after January 6, when the long Christmas break is over, and at the end of July and early August, before most stores close shop to take their August holidays. August is not the month to shop in Rome, it can be difficult enough to find an open restaurant, much less a shoe store. Stores that do remain open are usually geared exclusively to the tourist market, since locals are on holiday.

A new gimmick in Rome is the *vendita promozionale* (promotional sale), which can be presented in a variety of forms. Many are honest clearance sales; some are testing grounds for coming sales; others are smoke screens, with sales on a few current products but mostly on outdated items that have been gathering dust.

The secret to wise shopping in Rome is basically knowing what is stylish and what is passé. Decide what you want, and don't be in a hurry to purchase it the very first time you see it.

Unfortunately, time is against the traveler, who may not have the time to make a reconnaissance tour of prime shopping areas at sales times to compare prices.

Your best bet is to keep a keen eye on shop windows while you're touring or taking an evening stroll—so that when you're ready to shop you'll have some context for the prices you see.

STORE HOURS

Rome stores generally are open 9 A.M. to 1 P.M. and 3:30 to 7:30 P.M. in winter, 4 to 8 P.M. in summer. Tuesday through Saturday. Stores close on Sundays and for one half-day during the week. Clothing and apparel stores, jewelers, gift shops, and so forth close Monday morning; department stores generally remain open. Food stores close Thursday afternoon; hardware, paint stores, and the like close Saturday afternoon. During the summer months this half-day closing schedule is abandoned, and all stores close Saturday afternoon. Some stores have opted for the *orario unico,* and are open from 9 A.M. until 6 P.M. without the *siesta* break. All stores are obliged to post the hours they are open where they can easily be seen by the public.

Efforts have been made to extend late-evening shopping hours until 10 P.M. This met with mixed results last year; no clear policy is certain for 1989.

Shopping Areas

The prime shopping area in Rome is along **Via dei Condotti** and **Via Frattina** from **Via del Corso** to **Piazza di Spagna.** This is the area where most of the prime names in Italian fashion are quartered. This is also the high-rent district (with corresponding prices), so check out the shops on the area's perimeter, where the range of products may not be as vast, but prices are often lower than a block or two away.

The upper area of **Via del Corso** towards Piazza del Popolo has an abundance of shops catering to youthful whims and kitsch crazes. This same is true for most of **Via Nazionale,** especially the lower portion after the Quirino Theater. Occasional exceptions can be found around the intersection of Via Nazionale and Via delle Quattro Fontane.

The upper half of **Via Veneto** is noted for high prices, but often offers surprises. Since Arab oil money emanates from the first-class hotels around the Veneto, Middle Eastern, European, and North American concepts of chic can clash, but at least display windows here are well lit into the late evening, offering an opportunity to compare prices during a stroll.

In the vicinity is the high-rent but high-quality **Via Barberini,** extending from Piazza Barberini to Via Bissolati. This is also the major airline offices area.

Across the Tiber from Piazza del Popolo is **Via Cola di Rienzo,** which records one of the highest volumes of business in the capital. Most of the shops are found west of Piazza Cola di Rienzo to Piazza del Risorgimento, halfway between St. Peter's and the Vatican Museums. These privately owned shops usually have concession arrangements with leading stylists; the shop owner is generally on the premises, and amenable to "rounding off" prices on larger purchases, which can amount to a small savings.

In the monumental area around the **Pantheon** small shops alternate with restaurants, caffès, and sweets shops; keep an eye peeled for bargains. Around the **Trevi Fountain** avid competition flourishes between economy-class shoe stores for those who have been scared off by exorbitant prices in the Veneto and Piazza di Spagna areas (these prices are often up to twenty percent less than prices in Florence, the backyard for Tuscan shoe factories, since the abundance of stores in Rome has created a more competitive market).

An area not to be ignored by the serious shopper is the beginning of the **Via Appia Nuova** at Porta San Giovanni. This is where the Coin department store is located, and the number of shops on both sides of Via Appia Nuova down to Piazza Re di Roma is impressive. The area is making a serious effort to rival more centrally located competition, and can offer especially attractive sales.

Open-Air Markets

There are a number of open-air markets throughout Rome. Every section of Rome offers a similar market on a smaller scale. All attract *ambulanti*—roving vendors who rotate around five or six market areas across the city. Their goods can vary from factory rejects (a rare commodity in Italy) to a store's entire leftover inventory after *saldi* season. These sales are usually conducted by weight, and the sidewalk vendor can then offer vastly reduced prices.

Appearances can often be deceiving. Some of the stubble-chinned vendors who appear on the verge of starvation are often well-traveled entrepreneurs who import directly from India or China, and who simply prefer a more independent lifestyle to the confines of a store. **Piazza Vittorio** offers the largest fruit and vegetable market, with a scattering of stalls offering meats, *insaccati,* fish, and fowl.

The granddaddy of Rome's open-air markets is found every Sunday morning along the stretch of Via Portuense from **Porta Portese** to the underpass that leads into Piazza della Radio. Including the stalls on the side streets there are nearly two miles of stands, selling everything from used cars to newly born pups.

Of the estimated 2,200 vendors, only nine hundred have regular city licenses. The ever-increasing size of the Porta Portese Sunday-only market has sparked protests from area residents who want the city to move the market elsewhere. The city has expressed a willingness to consider the move if another suitable site can be found for this Roman tradition, as much a folk fair as a simple market.

The Porta Portese market is a haven for pickpockets, purse snatchers, and shell games—take precautions. Though the area is patrolled by city police, they are outnumbered.

In addition to the traditional fare of alleged antiques, spare parts for out-of-stock old motors and electric appliances, cheap clothes and leather goods, stamps, coins, and prints, there is now an international element in the market. African and Arab peddlers offer native handicrafts, carpets, and similar items that can also be found for sale throughout the city on sidewalks in a number of well-trafficked areas. Russian and Iranian refugees and other emigrants offer goods for sale when their funds are low. This is where serious bartering enters the scene, since such items often have personal value to the vendor.

The umbrella-covered **Via Sannio** market, behind the Coin department store at the San Giovanni metro A line stop, can offer tremendous bargains in leather goods and accessories. Here the asking price is never paid, and a sharp-eyed comparison shopper who is prepared to wrangle can get a good deal.

Department Stores

Rome's department stores range from the Coin and Rinascente to UPIM and Standa. Of these, Rinascente makes serious attempts to attract the foreign shopper, with such incentives as flat 10 percent discounts upon presentation of a passport (even with charge purchases) and money-changing services if purchases are made with traveler's checks. Some prices occasionally are also posted in U.S. dollars, at a very advantageous exchange rate.

Coin is in Piazzale Appio at Porta San Giovanni.

Rinascente is in Piazza Colonna and Piazza Fiume.

The **UPIM** locations at Via Nazionale 211, Piazza Santa Maria Maggiore, and Via del Tritone 172 are the most centrally located of their 17 outlets in Rome.

Standa's locations at Via Cola di Rienzo 173/181, Viale di Trastevere 60/64, and Via Appia Nuova 181/183 are among the most accessible of Standa's 36 Rome outlets.

International Designers

Giorgio Armani, Via del Babuino 102, tel. (06) 6793777, and **Emporio Armani,** Via del Babuino 140, tel. (06) 6788454, sell clothing for men and women, with Emporio Armani offering a more affordable end of the collection.

Benetton, Via dei Condotti 59, tel. (06) 6797982, and Via Cola di Rienzo 225, are just a few of the hundreds of outlets throughout the city for men's and women's clothing.

Brioni, Via Barberini 75/83; tel. (06) 484517.

Bulgari, Via dei Condotti 70, tel. (06) 6793876, is home base for the most internationally acclaimed jeweler in Rome.

Fendi, Via Borgognona 39, tel. (06) 6797641, sells leather and fur that needs no introduction.

Salvatore Ferragamo, Via dei Condotti 66 and 73/74, tel. (06) 6781130, is the Rome base for the famous Florentine cobbler. Ladies' apparel and accessories are also sold.

Gianfranco Ferre is at Via Borgognona 8, tel. (06) 6797445 and 42 B, tel (06) 6790050, also at Via Condotti 77, (06) 6796147; the Milanese fashion school keeps expanding its Rome base.

Richard Ginori, with stores at Via Cola di Rienzo 223, tel. (06) 352138, Via dei Condotti 87/90, tel. (06) 6784151, and Via del Tritone 177, tel. (06) 6793836, sells quality porcelain, ceramics, and crystal.

Gucci, Via dei Condotti 8, tel. (06) 6789340, is, of course, one of the most popular international names in leather goods.

Krizia is at Piazza di Spagna 77/8, tel. (06) 6793419; her castle outside Rome testifies to the popularity of this women's designer.

Bruno Magli sells men's and ladies' shoes at Via del Gambero 1, tel. (06) 6793802, Via Barberini 94, tel. (06) 486850, Via Veneto 70A, tel. (06) 464355, Via Cola di Rienzo 237, tel. (06) 351972.

Missoni offers colorful knits at Via Borgognona 38B, tel. (06) 6797971; for men only at Piazza di Spagna 78, tel. (06) 6792555; and for women only at Via del Babuino, tel. (06) 679791.

Luisa Spagnoli locations at Via Veneto 130, tel. (06) 465881, Via Frattina 116, tel. (06) 6795517, Via del Corso 385, tel. (06) 6793983, and Via Barberini 84, (06) 460757, are main outlets in central Rome for the Perugia women's stylist.

Stefanel has a dozen Rome outlets; the most central are Via Frattina 31/32, tel. (06) 6792667; Via Cola di Rienzo 191/193, tel. (06) 352954; and Via Nazionale 227, tel. (06) 485914.

Valentino's high-fashion center is at Via Gregoriana 24; tel. (06) 67391. Women's wear is at Via Bocca di

Leone 15/18; and men's clothing at Via Mario dei Fiori 22 (corner of Via dei Condotti); tel. (06) 6783656.

Mario Valentino at Via Frattina 58, tel. (06) 6791242, and Via Frattina 84, tel. (06) 6791246, represent the Neapolitan leather stylist.

Gianni Versace sells Milanese styling in Rome at Via Bocca di Leone 27; tel. (06) 6780521. There's also a store at Via Borgognone 29; tel. (06) 6795292.

Fabrics
Cesari, is at Via del Babuino 16, tel. (06) 3611441; linen and lingerie can also be found in the shop at Via Barberini 1; tel. (06) 463035.

Fallani, Via Vitelleschi 20/24 and 28/32, tel. (06) 6542652, also sells linen, men's and women's wear, and lingerie at wholesale prices, near the Vatican.

Polidori is at Via dei Condotti 21; tel. (06) 6784842.

Jewelry and Silverware
Bezzi, Via Colonna 43, tel. (06) 3604800, is run by the Bezzi brothers—they compete with the women in the family, who have set up a shop called **Giannotti 1880** at Lungotevere Mellini 44, Scala Valadier; tel. (06) 321399. Both are conveniently located in Prati, near the Vatican.

Fornari, Via dei Condotti 80, tel. (06) 6794285, is a Rome byword for quality silverware. Fornari also sells jewelry.

Giansanti, Via Sicilia 40; tel. (06) 493594—Carlo is gracious and accommodating in this reliable shop just off the Via Veneto. Custom orders are filled by experienced goldsmiths.

Leather Goods
Pier Caranti, Piazza di Spagna 43, tel. (06) 6791621, sells bags, belts, and briefcases.

Di Cori, Piazza di Spagna 53, tel. (06) 6784439, sells gloves.

Volterra, Via Barberini 102/104, tel. (06) 4819315, has quality luggage and men's and ladies' apparel.

Valigeria Romana, Via Silla 51; tel. (06) 318437. Besides making trunks and luggage, this is the Samsonite concessionaire in Rome, and repairs are made on luggage that has succumbed to the ordeals of international travel.

Shoes
FOR MEN AND WOMEN
Raphael Salato, Piazza di Spagna 34, tel. (06) 6795646; Via Veneto 149, tel. (06) 493507; or Via Veneto 104, tel. (06) 484677.

Trancanelli, Piazza Cola di Rienzo 84, tel. (06) 6878753; the store at Via Sabotino 52, tel. (06) 319156, sells the same shoes for less money.

Clothes
FOR MEN
For Man, Via Cola di Rienzo 184; tel. (06) 6874661.

Gaj, Piazza Cola di Rienzo 120/122; Aldo's wife has **Vedette** for the ladies next door at number 116/118.

Red and Blue, Via Due Macelli 57/58, just off Piazza di Spagna; tel. (06) 6791933.

Testa, Via Frattina 104, tel. (06) 6791298; and Via Borgognona 13, tel. (06) 6796174.

Uomo In, Via A. Regolo 15; tel. (06) 3598363.

Volpi, Via Barberini 76.

FOR WOMEN
DiPorto, Via Cola di Rienzo 186.

Max Mara, Via Frattina 28, tel. (06) 6793683; Via dei Condotti 46, tel. (06) 6787946; and a new location at Via Cola di Rienzo 275.

FOR YOUNG MEN
Antinco Caffè Moda, Via Genova 12, tel. (06) 4743323; also sells unisex clothing just off Via Nazionale.

FOR YOUNG WOMEN
Cipria, Via Ottaviano 58/64, is just down from the metro A line terminal on the way to the Vatican.

FOR CHILDREN

Chicco, Via della Penna 13/19 (just off Piazza del Popolo).

   Cicogna, Via Frattina 138, tel. (06) 6791912; Via Cola di Rienzo, tel. (06) 6530557.

   Raphael Junior, Via Veneto 98; tel. (06) 465692.

Gifts

Cose così, Via Candia 75A, tel. (06) 352184, offers a wide assortment of gifts at reasonable prices; it's near the Ottaviano metro stop on the A line. (Via Candia is the extension of Viale Giulio Cesare.)

Factory Outlets

Serious shoppers who are traveling elsewhere in Italy should stop at the I.C.E., the Italian Institute for Foreign Trade (Istituto Nazionale per il Commercio con l'Estero), Via Listz 21; tel. (06) 59921. Near the EUR Marconi metro stop on the B line, this is a government agency promoting Italian products, and can provide merchandise lists of factory outlets that include names, addresses, and telephone numbers of factories throughout the country. This may be a bit ambitious for the average tourist, but since it's along the walk to the Roman Civilization Museum, a stop may be worth the effort a week or so later when touring Tuscany, Veneto, the Marches, and other areas.

8

RESTAURANTS

If you think Rome hotels are expensive, wait until you try the restaurants. But first impressions can be misleading, because what constitutes a full meal for one in Rome would feed two anywhere else. *Antipasto* is followed by pasta or soup; then comes the *secondo* (second) course of meat, fowl, or fish followed by fruit, cheese, or a sweet. You are not obligated (or expected) to order everything (even though some waiters may give it a try).

Have a good breakfast and a light lunch as a break from sightseeing. It is all but impossible to eat before 7:30 P.M., so return to your hotel for a shower, and then stop at a sidewalk caffè for an *aperitivo*. By then it's restaurant time, and you'll be ready to enjoy a full Roman meal.

An old saying in Rome is that the rich are never hungry. But although servings may seem meager in the more expensive restaurants, a plate of pasta in a picturesque Trastevere trattoria can be overwhelmingly ample. Roman cuisine is not for weight watchers. It is hardy and tasty, and requires a chilled Frascati or another Albani Hills wine to stave off after-dinner thirst. The famous pasta dish *spaghetti alla carbonara* is actually Roman soul food modified. After World War II a black GI added an egg yoke or two to the heavily peppered spaghetti with bacon bits. His idea caught on, and *presto,* the foreign encroachment was complete.

Roman cooking makes heavy use of legumes, oxtails, entrails, spices, and pasta. Meat specialties are *abbacchio* (lamb) and *porchetta* (roast pig). Many restaurants feature fish despite rising costs; remember the menu's *etto* price refers to each 100 grams of weight (about four ounces) and not the price of the dinner.

Service is not a strong point in even the fancier Roman restaurants, so don't expect miracles in the more economical spots. If you have difficulty in getting your check, just stand up and head for the door—this usually gets results.

Foreign fare is abundant in Rome. The invasion of Chinese restaurants has seemingly emptied Peking. And of course, Rome has many restaurants featuring every other region in Italy. These pages include a good cross section of all, with foreign fare listed separately.

The monumental area has many offerings. Trastevere has an impressive concentration of large, small, expensive, and economical restaurants and trattorias. Good neighborhood spots usually run about Lit. 30,000 for a full meal with house wine. In Rome you can eat just as well or just as poorly as anywhere else. As fame increases, so does the tab; this should be remembered in selecting a restaurant. Listings include a neighborhood code for easy reference.

Prices given below are for a complete meal for one person, from antipasto to dessert. Credit cards are listed as accepted. "All cards" means that all of the following are accepted: AE—American Express; DC—Diner's Club; MC—MasterCard; V—Visa.

Neighborhood keys refer to page number of color map insert and the map coordinates at which restaurant is located.

🍷 THE SELECTIONS

EXPENSIVE

Ai Tre Scalini ARCHAEOLOGICAL ROME, P. 7, E4

Via SS. Quattro 30; tel. (06) 732695. Rossana and Matteo add a gastronomical touch to the best daily market produce, making a trip to the Colosseum even more enjoyable. A 5-min. walk behind the amphitheater, the restaurant is in a picturesque part of old Rome. Try the ravioli with goat cheese. Meals run Lit. 65,000. Closed Sat. noon, Sun. evening, Mon., July, Aug. All cards.

Alberto Ciarla TRASTEVERE, P. 6, C4

Piazza San Cosimato 40; tel. (06) 5818668. On the rim of the largest open-air produce market in the heart of popular Trastevere, the menu has a solid accent on fish, with aquariums displaying the menu offerings—fresh, fresh, fresh. Besides a good Italian and French wine list, Alberto offers a Bianco di Velletri Vigna Ciarla from the family vineyards. The *pasta e fagioli* soup with shellfish is first-class and a fine first course. No air conditioning, but outdoor tables in the summer. The waiters seem to be always undergoing on-the-job training. Meals run Lit. 80,000–100,000. Closed Sun., Aug. 5–25, Dec. 23–Jan. 10. All cards.

Fabrizio TRASTEVERE, P. 6, B3

Via Santa Dorotea 15; tel. (06) 5806244. Raised in the best of old Trastevere tradition, Fabrizio has chosen a more ambitious cooking path. Neptune reigns here, under Fabrizio's watchful eye; he personally selects each day's offerings from the fish stalls at Fiumicino. Traditional Roman dishes are also served, but the best are imaginative creations like *pasta e fagioli* with cuttlefish. Meals run Lit. 65,000. Closed Sun., Aug. 8–31. AE, MC.

Giggetto er Pescatore PARIOLI

Via Sant'Elia, Fonte dell'Acqua Acetosa; tel. (06) 679311. Located in a well-shaded area with ample parking, the restaurant has a good selection of seafood. A full meal can be an evening-long treat, but unfortunately the help sometimes can be moody and shuffling. Meals run Lit. 80,000. Closed Sun., last half of Aug. AE, DC.

Hostaria dell'Orso MONUMENTAL ROME, P. 2, C2

Via dei Soldati 25; tel. (06) 6864250. Open only in the evening, this 15th-century former inn often has an elite gathering at its ground-floor watering hole, where the subdued lighting makes it hard to see anyone. The elegant, refined restaurant on the first floor is perfect for romantic occasions, with background piano music to set the mood. The gracious service is a forgotten commodity in most of Rome, and it's air-conditioned, too. The food caps an evening to be remembered; try oysters au gratin with spinach sauce. Reservations recommended. (If the rafters creak under an occasional after-10 P.M. stomp, it's the second-floor disco coming to life.) Meals run Lit. 90,000. Closed Sun. All cards.

Mimi VATICAN, P. 2, B2

Via G. Belli 59; tel. (06) 3210962. The best restaurant on the isle of Ponza (off the southern coast of Lazio) is well represented in Rome by this elegant, intimate little restaurant, offering seafood specialties just around the corner from Piazza Cavour and the Palace of Justice. Table telephones ensure privacy. Meals are Lit. 65,000. Closed Mon. AE, DC. In Ponza, Mimi is on Via dietro la Chiesa, tel. (0771) 80338, and remains open seven days a week for the entire summer season. Seafood is less expensive here; meals run Lit. 50,000. Closed Mon. AE, DC.

Papà Giovanni

MONUMENTAL ROME, P. 2, C3

Via dei Sediari 4; tel. (06) 6565308. Just off Piazza Navona. Renato Sentuti has an avid local following for his creative use of what produce each season provides. Fully realizing the maxim that "the eye deserves its share," the choreography of a tried and talented hand is most apparent in his salads. Renato's sherbets are true and tasty. Dinners run Lit. 70,000–80,000. Closed Sun., Aug. All cards.

If the tab is a bit exorbitant, Renato's wife, Marisa, has her own little place, **G.B. Il Cardinale,** Via delle Carceri 6; tel. (06) 6569336. Kosher and Roman specialties are an abbreviation of Giovanni's fare. A dinner here costs Lit. 40,000–45,000. Closed Sun., Aug., AE.

Patrizia e Roberto del Pianeta Terra

MONUMENTAL ROME, P. 2, C3

Via Arco del Monte 94/95; tel. (06) 6869893. This little oasis of culinary creativity is tucked into a side street between Campo dei Fiori and Via Arenula, behind the Justice Ministry. Open only in the evening and with only 30 settings (so reservations are a must), it is one of the leading new-wave restaurants, which are becoming increasingly popular. Let Patrizia call the signals for ex-rugby-player husband Roberto in the kitchen. Meals run Lit. 75,000. Closed Sun., Aug. 8–28. AE, DC, MC.

Pino e Dino

MONUMENTAL ROME, P. 2, C3

Piazza di Montevecchio 22; tel. (06) 6861319. Off the Piazza Navona, this spot has had the same name for years, but not the same principals. Now it's Peppino and Tonino who are equally devoted to serving a panorama of Italy's cuisines. Here is positive proof that there is no one all-embracing style of Italian cooking. An elegant and intimate atmosphere in the evening relaxes to become suitable for a working lunch. At noon expect to pay around Lit. 35,000; for dinner, about Lit. 60,000. Closed Mon., 1 week in Aug., 3 in Jan. AE, DC.

Quinzi and Gabrielli

Via delle Coppelle 5; tel. (06) 6879389. Open for dinner only, 8 P.M.–midnight, but this little oyster bar is a local favorite. Elegant and intimate, with a few outdoor tables in the summer. A limited wine list reflects the same discerning eye that supervises the daily trip to the fish market. Dinner costs about Lit. 100,000. Closed Sun., Aug. AE, DC.

Ranieri

Via Mario dei Fiori 26; tel. (06) 6791592. Mario and Giovanni Forti are regaining the fame that once made this one of the best restaurants in the center of Rome (near the Piazza di Spagna). Founded by Neapolitan Giuseppe Ranieri, who was chef to England's Queen Victoria, the restaurant offers old world atmosphere to an army of foreign shoppers and tourers, but now the Italians are beginning to return. Specialties include spinach and ricotta cannellone, melanzana parmigiano, and a wide assortment of meat and fowl. Meals run Lit. 60,000 Closed Sun., 2 weeks in Aug. All cards.

San Souci

Via Sicilia 20; tel. (06) 4456194. Serving dinner only, this ultraelegant restaurant half a block off the Via Veneto is also ultrasmall. Reservations are necessary to assure a table. Have an *aperitivo* in the small lounge after descending into the restaurant, and take the opportunity to contemplate the mixed menu of nouvelle cuisine and inviting Italian fare. Fine crystal, porcelain, and linen and soft music complete a delightful atmosphere. Air-conditioned. Meals run Lit. 80,000–100,000. Closed Mon., Aug. All cards.

MODERATELY PRICED

Ambasciata d'Abruzzo

Via Pietro Tacchini 26; tel. (06) 878256. This air-conditioned restaurant is a favorite with foreign tourists. *Antipasto* is a basket of Abruzzo *insaccati,* ham, and cheese. A full meat meal runs Lit. 35,000, but can climb to Lit. 40,000 with fish. Closed Sun., 3 weeks in Aug. When the "embassy" is closed in summer, son Roberto's **Vicariato d'Abruzzo,** Via delle Fornaci 8/10; tel. (06) 633438, fills the gap with a similar dining experience and identical prices. Closed Mon. All cards at both.

Rooftop Dining

Charles, Hotel Eden, Via Ludovisi 49; tel. (06) 4742401. When the name of a hotel's restaurant derives from its maître d', the service has to be good. Soft music accompanies beautiful views from atop this hotel between the Via Veneto and Piazza di Spagna. The tab runs Lit. 80,000–100,000, but you can stop in for just a drink until midnight, for an unforgettable nightcap. Closed Sun., Aug. All cards.

Les Etoiles, Atlante Star Hotel, Via Vitelleschi 34; tel. (06) 6879558. It's difficult to imagine that this 5-star hotel was once a *pensione* with a fleet of roadside hustlers soliciting foreigners entering Rome on the old consular roads. Over 25 years the pensione took over the entire building and became a hotel that was associated with the Best Western chain, before renovating its way to luxury class. The roof garden offers a fine view of St. Peter's and Rome from the other side of the Tiber. Meals run Lit. 80,000. All cards.

Forum Roof-Garden, Hotel Forum, Via Tor dei Conti 28; tel. (06) 6792446. Most exciting is the overview of the main archaeological section of ancient Rome. Food, wine, and service are pleasant, but come here for the atmosphere; you'll have no doubt as to what city you're in. Meals run Lit. 70,000. All cards.

Hassler Roof-Garden, Hassler Villa Medici Hotel, Piazza Trinitá dei Monti 6; tel. (06) 6782651. Atop the Spanish Steps, this elegant, refined, air-conditioned restaurant has a beautiful view of monumental Rome. Service is impeccable and helps create a luxurious dining atmosphere. Meals average Lit. 120,000–135,000. All cards.

La Pergola, Cavalieri Hilton, Via Cadlolo 101; tel. (06) 31511. Open for dinner only, this is probably the best restaurant on the list. Rome will be at your feet from this Monte Mario perch. From the *degustazione* to *alla carta* alternatives, the tab can run Lit. 70,000–110,000. Closed Sun.; first 3 weeks of Jan. All cards.

Andrea   VIA VENETO AREA, P. 3, D2
Via Sardegna 26; tel. (06) 493707. With wife Francesca running the kitchen, Aldo De Cesare has guided this com-

fortable, air-conditioned restaurant into the limelight with some of the area's most tempting *antipasti,* fish, sweets, and wines. The crispy, plain pizza bread is rushed hot from the wood oven of the pizzeria across the street. The high demand at dinner and for business lunches means reservations are essential. Meals run Lit. 60,000. Closed Sun., Aug. 10–30. All cards.

Antico Romagnolo
ARCHAEOLOGICAL ROME, P. 3, D3

Via Panisperna 231; tel. (06) 4740620. In the 1930s this was a favorite meeting place for Italy's famed "boys of Via Panisperna," the group of physicists who included Enrico Fermi, Pontecorvo, Majorana, Amaldi, and Segré. Renovated by ex-Alitalia stewards Giacomo Ramenghi and Lino Menegon, but maintaining a comfortable old osteria air, the restaurant provides a vast assortment of regional dishes to satisfy practically any desire. There's an especially good antipasto spread; for your *secondo,* try *faraona* (guinea hen) breast with peppers. Meals run Lit. 30,000–35,000. Closed Sat. noon, Sun. AE, DC, V.

Il Caminetto
PARIOLI

Viale Parioli 89; tel. (06) 803946. Air-conditioned inside for lunch, dinner is served outside during the summer. A comfortable, neighborhood restaurant with a fine panorama of regional cuisine. You'll find a good antipasto spread and a wide assortment of pastas, always al dente. Meals run Lit. 35,000–40,000. Closed Thurs., 1 week in mid-Aug. AE, DC, MC.

La Carbonara
MONUMENTAL ROME, P. 6, C3

Piazza Campo dei Fiori 23; tel. (06) 6864783. On a characteristic market square just a block from the Farnese Palace, this favorite with the most Roman of Rome politicians, as well as visiting Soviets, offers open-air dining on the square in summer. But make sure the street cleaners are not on strike, otherwise.... Roman specialties and a good variety of pastas are on the menu. Expect dinner to run Lit. 40,000. Closed Thurs., Aug. 10–30. AE.

Dante
VATICAN, P. 1, B2

Taberna dei Gracchi, Via dei Gracchi 266/268; tel. (06) 383757. Dante Mililli's success story since abandoning an old Trastevere eatery 26 years ago is reflected in every corner of this modern, air-conditioned restaurant. But Dante has remained faithful to his old Trastevere roots, and serves as a Roman gastronomical ambassador abroad, in London, Berlin, and New York (at Girafe, 208 E. 58th St.). In Rome, customers include printers who have remained faithful over the years, the Lazio professional soccer team, attorneys, judges, and tourists from neighboring first-class hotels. Meals run Lit. 45,000–50,000. Closed Sun., Mon., noon, Aug. 5–25. AE, DC, V.

On the Tiber

The old *Roman Holiday* barge of Audrey Hepburn and Gregory Peck today is no more than a burned-out hull on the banks of the Tiber. The river is so polluted that swimming is prohibited; a sip of its waters would be lethal. But riverside dining can still be attractive. Two possibilities both have sun decks for tanning buffs.

Il Canto del Riso, under Ponte Cavour (enter by the stairs across from Lungotevere Mellini 7); tel. (06) 3610430. Alvaro Silvestri is an authentic boat person, but a pragmatic one. The riverside Canto features rice first courses and seafood seconds. Meals average Lit. 30,000–40,000. Closed Sun. evening, Mon., Nov. 1–March 31. No cards.

Isola del Sole, Lungotevere Arnaldo da Brescia; tel. (06) 3601400. Giulio Bendandi's barge restaurant is open year-round, though it closes at high tide. Reservations are a must for the 1–3 P.M. lunch and 8:30–11:30 P.M. dinner. Meals run Lit. 35,000–40,000. Closed Mon. AE.

Sister Clelia manages **Isola del Sole No. 2** (also known as al Khadir) at Porto Ercole, Via dei Cannoni 4, Banchina Santa Barbara; tel. (0546) 831248. Prices run Lit. 40,000–50,000. No cards.

Fortunato
MONUMENTAL ROME, P. 2, C3
Via del Pantheon 55; tel. (06) 6792788. Near the Pantheon, between the Senate and Chamber of Deputies, this restaurant attracts Parliamentarians. Fresh fish is guaranteed every day, as well as vegetables that are a house specialty, spaghetti with clams, and *gnocchi*. Ricotta cheese is featured in crepes and a rustic Roman pie. Expect to pay Lit. 40,000–50,000 for dinner. Closed Sun., Aug. 10–31. AE.

Giovanni
VIA VENETO AREA, P. 3, E2
Via Marche 19; tel. (06) 493576. The Sbrega family under-taking specializes in the most typical Italian dishes with a deft touch. Sports and entertainment personalities are among a faithful local clientele, bolstered by visitors from north and south. Meals run Lit. 50,000–55,000. Closed Fri. evening, Sat., Aug. AE, V.

Girone VI
MONUMENTAL ROME, P. 2, C3
Vicolo Sinibaldi 2; tel. (06) 6542831. In a picturesque alley off Via del Torre Argentina, 5 min. from the Pantheon, is Gabriele and Antonietta Oreggia's elegant little restaurant in a 15th-century crypt. The seven tables inside are bol-stered by another four or five in the alley during the sum-mer. Open evenings only, 8 P.M.–midnight, year-round. A former Alitalia flight steward, Gabriele is aided by son Marco, an aspiring sommelier, in adding an appealing per-sonal touch to old Italian recipes. When you leave you're almost one of the family. Dinner runs Lit. 55,000. Closed Sun., 10 days over Christmas. AE, MC, V.

Grottino
VATICAN
Via Oslavia 54; tel. (06) 3612703. A little beyond the Vati-can's perimeter, but the husband-wife team of Alfredo and Alberta Fiorio hosts an elegant, air-conditioned, totally ren-ovated basement restaurant featuring the renaissance of traditional recipes with an inventive flare. The menu changes nightly; but try the linguine with crab meat if avail-able. Going into its second year, the restaurant already draws heavily from the nearby radio and television studios. Meals run Lit. 35,000. Closed Sun., Aug. 10–20. AE, V.

Piazza Navona

Two restaurants that take advantage of incredible locations on one of the most beautiful piazzas in Europe are **Mastrostefano,** Piazza Navona 94/100; tel. (06) 6542855 (closed Mon., Jan 10–27, Aug. 18–31), and **Tre Scalini,** Piazza Navona 30; tel. (06) 6861234 (closed Wed). Tabs at both can orbit up to Lit. 50,000–60,000, in-cluding wine. Both take all cards. Make reservations for an outdoor table and feast your eyes on Bernini's Fountain of Four Rivers. But be aware that it's the atmosphere, not the food you're paying for.

Il Matriciano
VATICAN, P. 1, B2
Via dei Gracchi 55; tel. (06) 3212327. Next to the area's largest city market, Giuseppe Colasanti's traditional fare can be appreciated until midnight. Tables can flow onto the sidewalks in warmer weather, and it is better to reserve a table in advance. Obliging waiters are ready to advise on a vast assortment of selections that include regional and classic specialties, including the pasta dish *buccattini* alla matriciana and grilled meats. Meals run Lit. 35,000–40,000. Closed Sat., Aug. 5–29. All cards.

Al Moro
MONUMENTAL ROME, P. 2, D2
Vicolo delle Bollette 13; tel. (06) 6783495. In its 60th year this restaurant near the Trevi Fountain is a little labyrinth of small rooms from various past expansions. Franco Romagnoli maintains a good dining tradition in the second generation. (His late father submitted to Federico Fellini's powers of persuasion to play a prime supporting role in *Satyricon,* between turns of directing waiters and the kitchen staff.) Here the *carbonara* is prepared with red peppers instead of black pepper. A steady clientele makes reservations a must. Air-conditioned. Meals run Lit. 45,000–50,000. Closed Sun., Aug. No cards.

Da Pancrazio
MONUMENTAL ROME, P. 6, C3
Piazza del Biscione 92; tel. (06) 6861246. There is outdoor dining on the small square just off Campo dei Fiori, but for atmosphere, romantics prefer the lower level inside, amid the ruins of the first-century B.C. Pompeo Theater, where Caesar was believed to have been assassinated. In such an atmosphere Roman specialties are a must, but the fish is also tempting. Dinners run Lit. 35,000–40,000. Closed Wed., Aug. 12–18. All cards.

Piperno
GHETTO, P. 6, C3
Monte dei Cenci 9; tel. (06) 6540629. In the heart of the old Jewish quarter, the air-conditioned restaurant's kosher cooking has an appeal that surpasses religious belief. Artichokes abound in the Roman countryside, and "Jewish style" *(alla giudiea)* is the way to order them in Rome. It is a house specialty here, along with a wide assortment of vegetable *antipasti* and baccala. Meals run Lit. 40,000–65,000. Closed Sun. evening, Mon., Aug. No cards.

Regno Sardo
VATICAN, P. 1, B1/2
Via Fabio Massimo 101; tel. (06) 3212501. It's been a long way from Ortueri, in Sardinia, for Giovanni Bonu, but since

he set up shop in an old osteria, that seemed to have seen the wrath of God, things have never been the same. Nowhere in Rome can a seafood spread—from antipasto to spaghetti with clams to a mixed, grilled seafood platter—be found at Giovanni's prices. He cuts corners elsewhere—and accommodates clients with a smile. The hurried, demanding, and pretentious should go elsewhere. For Giovanni, dinner in his restaurant is an evening to be enjoyed—relax and loosen your belt. Meals are Lit. 35,000–40,000 depending on wine. Closed Mon., Aug. 10–25. AE, DC, V.

Romolo a Porta Settimiana

TRASTEVERE, P. 5, B3

Via Porta Settimiana 8; tel. (06) 5818284. Legend has it that this was the osteria Raphael frequented while adorning the walls of the Farnese Palace. The exuberant master was attracted by a local barmaid. In succeeding generations the likes of Trilussa (Rome's favorite poet) and Guttuso (an acclaimed contemporary artist, who favored friend Romolo with a sketch for the menu) joined the rank and file of the famous who have passed these portals. The Casali clan has reigned since Romolo set up shop in 1923 in one of the most picturesque corners of old Rome. Daughter Marisa continues the tradition with the best of Roman cuisine and other regions' specialties. Ox-tail is a winter favorite. A large courtyard can accommodate 180 diners, but reservations are suggested. Meals are Lit. 45,000–55,000. Closed Mon., Aug. 5–29. AE, DC, V.

Sabatini in Trastevere

TRASTEVERE, P. 6, C4

Back-to-back are two restaurants in one: at Vicolo Santa Maria in Trastevere 18; tel. (06) 5818307 (closed Tues.), and at Piazza Santa Maria in Trastevere 13; tel. (06) 582026 (closed Wed.). Salvatore, Silvestro, and Francesco Sabatini continue one of the best traditions in Trastevere. The sober, intimate, labyrinthed interior is offset by outdoor summer dining on the square, opposite one of the more beautiful churches in Rome. Seafood occupies a prime role, but the principal fare is still traditional Roman, which couldn't have a more appropriate setting. For dinner on the square reservations are a must. Meals run Lit. 40,000–55,000. Both closed Aug. 14–17. All cards.

Trastevere

No one eats and runs in Trastevere; the experience is a leisurely evening in old Rome. The Trastevere food tradition could fill volumes, and high prices are not necessary. There still exist purely family-style *osterie* with paper-covered wooden tables; foreign food; fast food; gay bars; and cabarets. A stroll through the area between Santa Maria in Trastevere and Piazza San Cosimato, on the right of Viale di Trastevere, or from Piazza Sidney Sonnino to Piazza dei Mercanti on the left, will always turn up a pot luck alternative and a pleasant evening.

Osteria Santa Ana

MONUMENTAL ROME, P. 2, C1

Via della Penna 68/69; tel. (06) 3610291. Around the corner from Piazza del Popolo is a fine, elegant restaurant that offers good food in a pleasant atmosphere. Two steps down (watch your head) and you're almost in Osteria St. Ana (there's outside dining in warmer months). Here the best of Roman specialties, seafood, veal, and imaginative pasta courses follow an attractive antipasto cart. Meals run Lit. 45,000. Closed Sun., 2nd half Aug. All cards.

Trattoria Toscana al Girrarosto

VATICAN, P. 1, B2

Via Germanico 56; tel. (06) 314718. Roman fare is not exactly ignored, but the accent is decidedly Tuscan—Bruni's origin, menu, and wine list make this one of the most truly Tuscan eateries in the capital. Don't even try just walking in—reservations are a must for this restaurant, favorite among Vatican hierarchy. Meals are Lit. 45,000–60,000. Closed Mon., Aug. AE.

BASIC BARGAINS
Bella Napoli

VATICAN, P. 1, A1

Via S. De Saint Bon 59; tel. (06) 314712. Roman and Molise cuisine, seafood recipes, and good pizza from two young men who have renovated this old neighborhood eatery and smashed doubts that quality would suffer. The expansion and outdoor tables in summer can make service less than immediate, but the wait is worth the effort. The sauté di frutti di mare is exceptional. Weekend evenings are impossible without reservations. Meals are Lit. 25,000–30,000. Closed Mon., Aug. No cards.

Hosteria del 104

Via Urbana 104; tel. (06) 484556. This delightful little restaurant is a Sicilian-American effort featuring specialties from the native lands of both partners, plus some. Baked ham with pineapple, spaghetti with eggplant, Mexican chili, and lemon pie are a few. The daily menu is limited to several house specialties. You can expect a satisfying meal in this comfortable, clean, but small restaurant; reservations may be smart. A perfect lunch stop between Santa Maria Maggiore and the Colosseum, for Lit. 15,000. Dinners run Lit. 19,000, beverages extra. Closed Wed., Aug. AE.

Otello alla Concordia

Via della Croce 81; tel. (06) 6791178. A pleasant stop while shopping; take the last left off Piazza di Spagna before entering Via del Babuino. The narrow street of Via della Croce opens onto a pleasant courtyard where Otello successfully caters to foot-weary tourists and a clientele from the nearby art galleries and antique shops. A bowl of pasta and a salad make a satisfying lunch. Several set tourist menus with house wine are available. Dinners run Lit. 20,000–30,000. Closed Sun., 2 weeks at Christmas. AE.

Palmerie

Via Cimarra 4/5; tel. (06) 4744110. Reservations are a must in this little osteria with a steady clientele. A quick coat of paint, and Nicola and Beatrice Cerazoli joined the ranks of young couples in Rome who offer economical dining alternatives. A quick, light lunch featuring exotic salads (Tues.–Fri.) runs Lit. 20,000–25,000; dinner runs about Lit. 30,000. Closed Mon., Aug. 10–20. No cards.

LATE DINING/SNACKS

Rome evening dining is already late by U.S. and Northern European standards with most restaurants beginning service no earlier than 7:30 P.M. Service will be provided in most places until 10:30 or 11 P.M. After that it can become a bit tight. There are restaurants such as Girone VI (see above) that cater to the theater crowd, but reservations are required. The same is true for several places around the Sistina Theatre on Via Sistina and Via Federico Cesi.

Open around the clock is the **Risorgimento Restaurant** at Piazza Risorgimento 46, tel. 6569776, near the Vatican, offering everything from full meals to pizza. Here you'll be at one terminal of the all-night 30 tram. Not

FOREIGN FOOD

African: *Mar Rosso,* Via Conte Verde 62; tel. (06) 730702. Closed Tues.

Arab: *Taverna Negma,* Borgo Vittorio 92; tel. (06) 6565143. Closed Tues.

Austro-German: *Wiener Bierhaus,* Via della Croce 21; tel. (06) 6795569. Closed Wed.

Chinese: *Huang Cheng,* Via Santamaura 45/47; tel. (06) 353371. Closed Wed. *Lon Fon,* Via Firenze 44/46; tel. (06) 4755261. Closed Wed. *La Grande Muraglia,* Via. G. Tavani Arquati 107; tel. (06) 5816640. Closed Mon.

Egyptian: *La Piramide,* Viale di Porta Ardeatina 114; tel. (06) 5759880. Closed Mon. (Egyptian menu only Wed. and Thurs.)

French: *Chez Albert,* Via della Vaccarella 11; tel. (06) 6565549. Closed Sun.

Greek: *Dionisios,* Via della Pelliccia 4; tel. (06) 5803556. Open for dinner only. Closed Tues.

Indian: *India House,* Via Santa Cecilia 8; tel. (06) 5818508. Open for dinner only. Closed Mon.

Indonesian: *Bali,* Via del Mattonato 29; tel. (06) 5896089. Open for dinner only. Closed Mon.

Japanese: *Hamasei,* Via della Mercede 35/36; tel. (06) 6792134. Closed Mon.

Korean: *Han,* Borgo Angelico 26/30; tel. (06) 6547551. Closed Tues.

Latin American: *Asino Cotto,* Via del Vascellari 48; tel. (06) 5898985. Closed Mon.

Lebanese: *Sharazad,* Largo del Chiavari 83/84; tel. (06) 6564150. Closed Mon.

Mexican: *Messico e Nuvole,* Via Dei Magazzini Generali 8; tel. (06) 5741609. Dinner every night from 9 P.M., June–Oct.

Spanish: *El Patio,* Via Casilina 1108; tel. (06) 260201. Closed Wed.

Sri Lankan: *Lotus,* Via Vespasiano 25; tel. (06) 352073.

Tunisian: *Marcel,* Via della Scala 8; tel. (06) 5816317. Closed Sun.

Vietnamese: *Thien-Kim,* Via Giulia 201; tel. (06) 6547832. Closed Sun.

---

far away, if a light snack or freshly baked pastry is desired, is **Quelli della Notte** on Via Leone IV between Viale G. Cesare and Viale delle Milizie. Closed Mon. this gathering spot (no tables) for night owls is open from 10 P.M. to 7 A.M. Open to 3 A.M. are **le Nane,** Via Flaminia 527 (tel. 3280903) and **Domino's,** Via Lazio 22 (tel. 464689). Both feature hamburgers and pizzas as well as pasta, fish, and meat. It's just yours for the choosing. Le Nane is just before the Corso Francia bridge and is best reached by automobile. Domino's is just off the Via Veneto.

Then there are a number of off-beat places to be found around town offering snacks, exotic salads and a wide variety of foreign beers. As a rule these are open to 2 or 3 A.M. A few suggestions here are the **L'Asino Cotto,** Via del Vascellari 48, tel. 5898985 (closed Mon.) in Trastevere. Near the Pantheon, is **Hemingway,** Piazza delle Coppelle 10, tel. 6544135. Behind Piazza Navona there are **Giulio Passami l'Olio,** Via di Monte Giordano 26 (no phone) and **Il Merlo Maschio,** Via del Governo Vecchio 12, tel. 6861813, closed Mon. Near the Vatican are **Hungry Bogart,** Borgo Pio 202 (no phone) and **Tattoo,** Via degli Scipioni 238, tel. 319149. Some of the above places are a bit bare; some are private clubs that will require purchase of a membership card at Lit. 1–2,000 per person along with a tab of Lit. 10,000 to 15,000 for a snack and beer.

9

ENTERTAINMENT

Rome is far from being the entertainment capital of the Western world. And in August, there is more happening in the middle of the Dead Sea than in the stiflingly hot Eternal City.

In the Summer

The local tourist board (EPT) makes an admirable effort on the Isola Tiberina every evening, with games, music, snacks, and pizza stands to help you unwind after hours of walking in the sun or stuffy museums. (Air-conditioning is still considered a luxury by state and city officials.)

Discos, piano bars, jazz retreats, cabarets, theaters, and cinemas all close for a month or more. The more ambitious enterprises follow the beautiful people to the beach or the more fashionable mountain resorts and set up shop for the holiday. Those who do not close out of desperation—Rome's heat can be brutal in August.

The main musical attraction is the **summer open-air opera** season at the Baths of Caracalla. (See Baths of Caracalla in the sightseeing section for ticket information.) Most public bus service has terminated for the evening by the time the performance is over, but the city's ATAC provides a special fleet of buses to cover general routes into all main sections of the city to assure transportation for most of the way back to hotels. The EPT is working to secure the same service for its Isola Tiberina street fair when it ends at 1 A.M.

Another option for a summer evening is the only **English-language movie house,** Pasquino, at Vicolo dei Piedi 19; telephone (06) 5803622.

But if neither of the above appeals to you, it's best to join that untarnished Roman pastime, people watching.

When the city begins to repopulate in September, theater season manifests are posted, and the piano bars, discos, and cabarets return to the usual grind for another season.

People Watching

Gawking finds its maximum expression in Rome. The Via Veneto is most attractive during the day, when the shops are open. Here **Doney** and **Café de Paris** are old favorites, but there are less crowded perches such as **Carpano,** up a block towards the Porta Pinciana. During July or August, it's tourist watching tourist—almost like being back at JFK waiting for your flight to Europe.

Things are a bit brighter in Piazza Navona, or even the Pantheon. The street artists, fire-eaters, and other exhibitionists provide pleasant diversion while you're admiring Bernini's fountains. The popularity of caffès can change from year to year, but two favorites with tourists on Piazza Navona are **Tre Scalini,** which features a chocolate ice cream *tartufo* with bits of chocolate, and **Mastrostefano,** which offers a special *coppa gigante* that is a meal of ice cream and fruit cocktail. A comfortable little caffè that recently replaced an art gallery is the **Barberini,** in the end zone near the Fountain of Neptune.

A pleasant *passeggiata* (stroll) from Piazza Navona will take you across Corso Rinascimento into Piazza Sant'Eustacchio, for a creamy espresso at the **Caffè Sant'Eustacchio,** then on to Piazza della Rotonda (near the Pantheon), which attracts Roman youths. As a result, there are a never-ending number of caffès, bars, ice cream parlors, video bars, and so forth in the area. Stroll up around the Parliament's Chamber of Deputies in the evening, when traffic is quiet, to savor the real flavor of Rome.

The metro runs until 11:30 P.M. Although it's relatively safe, petty thievery is an ever-present possibility. Have a caffè call a cab for your return to your hotel, instead.

Clubs and Discos

Two discos that are especially popular with the young and young at heart are **Bella Blu,** Via Luciani 21; tel. (06) 3608840 (open 9 P.M. to 3:30 A.M.), and **Much More,** Via Luciani 52; tel. (06) 870504 (open 11 P.M. to 3 A.M., and also 4 to 8 P.M. Saturday and Sunday; closed Monday). These two spots have rejuvenated staid Parioli, to a point.

The **Jackie O',** Via Boncompagni 11; tel. (06) 461401 (open 11 P.M. to 3:30 A.M.; closed Monday), is just off the Via Veneto and convenient to area hotels. Phone for reservations, since the club is often used for private parties. Across the Via Veneto is the **Club 84,** Via Emilia 84; tel. (06) 4751538 (open 10 P.M. to 3:30 A.M.), another of the very few legitimate night spots in town.

Too many clubs have sidewalk hustlers who use every imaginable ploy to con singles into astronomical tabs, ruining the vacations of unsuspecting tourists.

The temple of Italian rock in the 1960s was the Piper Club. Now the **Piper '80,** Via Tagliamento 9, tel. (06) 854459, it still stages live shows to punctuate its more regular videos.

Piano Bars

Once upon a time (about twenty years ago) there was a young American following in the wake of two expatriates who had long been on the piano-bar scene in Paris, Bricktop and Charlie Beal. Bricktop had her own basement place on the Veneto, and Charlie entertained the nostalgic at the American-owned Luau, which used to be on the Via Sardegna, off Via Veneto.

The young man had his playing in order, but the Italians didn't give him much of a chance to prove his real worth. Finally he packed up, returned stateside, and achieved international success with the score for *Rocky.*

The likes of Bill Conti, Bricktop, and Charlie Beal are now missing from the Rome piano-bar scene. But who knows when another genius may wander in?

Every now and then Romano Mussolini, youngest son of the Fascist dictator, shows up at a piano with his lifelong passion for jazz.

For a casual drink and a few sounds, try:

Little Bar, Via Gregoriana 54A; tel. (06) 6796386. **Manuia,** Vicolo del Cinque 54; tel. (06) 58170716, features Brazilian music; there's a restaurant with a courtyard garden next door, so you can make it a complete evening without traveling very far. **La Prugna,** Piazza dei Ponziani 3; tel. (06) 5890555. **Tartarughino,** Via della Scrofa 2; tel. (06) 6786037, draws a crowd from Roman personalities.

Concerts, Theater, and Special Events

Rome has an active **concert season** from the fall to the beginning of summer. In June and into July concerts are staged in parks around the city, and there is **Jazz on a Tiber Barge** at Foro Italico, Italy's largest athletic complex, 15 minutes from the Prati area.

Rome has finally cracked the major rock-concert tours. Pink Floyd and Michael Jackson are just a few of the international favorites who played the Flaminio Stadium last year. The traveler's chance of obtaining tickets to big-name concerts unfortunately is likely limited to buying from scalpers the night of the concert.

For concerts, special events, and what-have-you, the entertainment section of the Rome daily *Il Messaggero* is probably the best list of happenings in Rome. Too often there is not much advance publicity for events.

Rome always draws a **circus** or two at Christmas. Though the Italian troupes may lack the kitsch that is common in the U.S., they provide an entertaining afternoon or evening. And there are generally visiting East European and Asian troupes which, with glasnost, may now find U.S. bookings.

Theater is naturally all in Italian, but musicals may at times be worth a trip to non-speakers of Italian for just the music and dance. Theater troupes take off Sunday evening and Monday. This can mean that a concert will be sandwiched into the theater's idle moment. Often foreign performers are featured, especially at the **Sistina,** Via Sistine 29; telephone (06) 4756841.

Sports

The sporting scene is dominated by the **soccer** season from September to May. Italy is preparing to host the 1990 World Cup tournament, and local heroes are being closely scrutinized along with the foreign stars who toil in the ranks of leading Italian teams.

Rome's two professional teams are Roma and Lazio. Between them they have captured only three Italian titles. But in recent years Roma has usually been a contender. Lazio has just returned to the A League in an interesting rotation formula that relegates one year's cellar dwellers to the B League, and promotes the top three teams of the B League to the A League. This always assures a lively battle for the league championship, and an elimination of complacency in the bottom of the standings among teams battling to remain in the major league.

League games are limited to Sunday; with both Rome teams in the A League, the city is practically assured a major-league game every week at the Olympic Stadium, Foro Italico. Italian Cup matches and friendlies (exhibition games) may be played during the week.

The national team should have a rich schedule of friendlies until cup time, since as tournament host Italy will not play in a qualification round.

You can take the number 911 bus to Foro Italico; there are also special buses running to and from the stadium on Sundays—but these tend to be outrageously crowded. Bars around the city sometimes sell tickets the week before the game.

Basketball is the second most popular sport in the country, and Italy probably has the world's highest-paid amateur players. Under the guise of industrial ball (teams sponsored by corporations), the Italian league attracts a number of U.S. players who had full careers in the NBA. And there is always a player or two who survived all but the final NBA team cut, and remains active in Italy in hopes of getting a second shot the next time around. Rome's Banco Roma team has enthusiastic followers who almost rival the frenzy that engulfs the more powerful northern teams. Home games are generally played at the Sports Palace that was constructed in EUR for the 1960 Olympic games. Take the metro B line.

This is also the arena for major **boxing** matches, but Rome is no longer the center of this sport in Italy; the recent death of promoter Rodolfo Sabatini left a tremendous void in local boxing organizations. Do-it-yourself enthusiasts won't be denied, but public boxing facilities are severely lacking. The gym scene is dominated by private clubs that often have difficulty in accommodating their own members.

In and around Rome there are two **horse,** one **dog,** and one **auto racing** circuit. Regular horse racing is near the Ciampino airport at the Capannelle, Via Appia Nuova, km. 12; telephone (06) 7993144; the **trotters** are at Tor di Valle, Via del Mare, km. 9; telephone (06) 6564129. To get to Capannelle, take the A line metro to the Colli Albani Stop and the ATAC bus 664 to the track. The trotters go under the lights, as do the dogs at the Ponte Marconi track near EUR, Via della Vasca Navale 6; telephone (06) 5566258.

Auto racing is twenty miles out on the Via Cassia at Valle Lunga; telephone (06) 9041417.

Il Corriere dello Sport is a daily sports newspaper in Rome that has complete information on activity at all of these tracks. The local racing form is *Il Cavallo,* for those who want to get serious. There is off-track betting in Italy, and a visit to a local betting shop will find characters even Damon Runyon never imagined.

Participant Sports

The largest **outdoor pool** and an **indoor pool** are in the Olympic Committee complex at Foro Italico, across the Tiber in northern Rome. Opening hours can vary, depending on scheduled lessons and competitions; telphone (06) 3601498 for specific information.

For active **tennis** enthusiasts attempts may be made to make reservations with the courts at EUR, Viale dell'Artigianato 2, telephone (06) 5924693; Foro Italico, Lungotevere Maresciallo Diaz, telephone (06) 3619021; the Tennis Club Belle Arti, Via Flaminia 158, telephone (06) 3600602; or the Tre Fontane complex near EUR, Via delle Tre Fontane, telephone (06) 5926386. Courts are very hard to come by; early morning times are your best bet.

For a round of **golf,** you must apply well in advance for a temporary membership with either of the two local clubs that have 18-hole courses: Acqua Santa, Via Appia Nuova 716, telephone (06) 783407; or Olgiata, Largo Olgiata 15, telephone (06) 3789141.

Bowlers can always find a lane with Enrico Vietri at the Bowling Brunswick, Lungotevere Acqua Acetosa; telephone (06) 3966696. To keep youngsters occupied, there is a wide assortment of video games. Facilities are smaller at Bowling Roma, at the more central Viale Regina Margherita 181; telephone (06) 861184.

The most complete **health club** in Rome is the Roman Sport Center, Via del Galoppatoio 33; telephone (06) 3601667. Adjacent to the underground parking facility in Villa Borghese, it is open from 8:30 A.M. to 11 P.M.

10

SHORT TRIPS OUT OF ROME

The overpowering presence of Rome can outshine many of the attractions elsewhere in the region of Lazio. But the Eternal City's mind-boggling abundance of monuments, fountains, museums, and art and artifacts can create the need for relief and relaxation, for the quaint, the calm, the picturesque. The Lazio countryside's minor provinces offer not-so-minor attractions that would be more prominent farther from Rome.

Anzio is now a popular beach resort 36 miles south of Rome. You can take ACOTRAL buses near the San Giovanni A line metro stop. On January 22, 1944, Anzio was where Anglo-American troops landed against weak German resistance, then camped while the Germans regrouped. Reminders of this Allied indecision are the 8,000 U.S. graves in nearby Nettuno and the 1,000 British graves in a cemetery along the road to Albano.

Best Beaches. The coast around Rome and most of Lazio is only for the most desperate beach buff. The best beach areas are at **Santa Marinella** (41 miles north of Rome on the Via Aurelia; you can take ACOTRAL buses from Viale Giulio Cesare) and **San Felice Circeo** (60 miles south of Rome on the Via Pontina). But the best suggestion is **Ponza** in the Pontine Islands. Ferry service is available from Anzio, Circeo, Terracina, and Formia. (Circeo, Terracina, and Formia are also served by ACOTRAL.) But don't go in August; if you're wondering why Rome is so deserted, you'll rapidly discover where everyone went when you arrive in Ponza.

If you're having difficulty conversing, try English. The local dialect is more an offshoot of Neapolitan, and difficult to understand; but many of the fishing folk and their families split their time between Ponza and Brooklyn.

✦ MANGIARE

South of Rome, along the way to the ferry port at Formia, a pleasant restaurant is **Italo,** Via Unita d'Italia, tel. (0771) 21529. A good, complete seafood meal with wine in this modern, seaside restaurant with summer dining terrace is Lit. 40,000. Closed Mon., Dec. 22–Jan. 5. AE, DC, V.

SIDETRIP TO GAETA

Below Formia on the coast is the town of Gaeta and its fortress-prison, where Nazi SS officers convicted for atrocities in Italy were incarcerated. One died after being taken out of a Rome military hospital in a suitcase; another was returned to Austria by then-Premier Bettino Craxi, in spite of public referendums explicitly against his release.

Cassino. Just south of Formia on the Via Appia is a good road (SS630) for the 35-mile drive to Cassino, a recommended stop on a drive through Lazio or to Naples. Cassino is on the SS6 Via Casilina, and just off the A2 Rome–Naples turnpike, at the base of the hilltop **Abbey of Montecassino,** the cradle of the Benedictine Order. Founded by St. Benedict in A.D. 529, the abbey was completely destroyed for the fourth time in 1944 by Allied bombing and artillery that sought to dislodge the German garrison that was controlling the roads to Rome. Fortunately for posterity, the abbey's rich historic archives had been transferred to the Vatican. Ironically, the abbey became more fortified by the destruction, as debris bolstered the massive walls. The view of Cassino is eerie, with its vacant lots marked only by the foundations of former houses, remaining as a reminder of the price of war paid by the civilian population. Free Polish forces led the attacks up the hill, and near an obelisk that commemorates the battle is a cemetery containing the remains of 1,100 Polish soldiers who helped to liberate the road to Rome.

The abbey is open to the public 7 A.M. to 12:30 P.M. and 3:15 P.M. to sunset. Under the high altar in the richly decorated basilica is an urn containing the remains of St. Benedict and his sister St. Scolastica. Both died here in A.D. 543.

Ostia Antica is 15 miles southwest of Rome on the Via del Mare to Ostia beach. The old Roman seaport can also be reached by train from Rome's Porta San Paolo station (to Ostiense). All of the **ruins** are open to a scorching summer sun, so wear a hat, or visit late in the afternoon. Open 9 A.M. to one hour before sunset. Closed Monday. Lit. 2000.

MANGIARE

Drive over to the fishing port of **Fiumicino** for dinner at **Bastianelli al Molo,** Via Torre Clementina 312; tel. (06) 6440118. One of the best seafood restaurants on the Roman coast. Dinner runs Lit. 40,000–60,000. Closed Mon. All cards.

Palestrina is 23 miles southeast of Rome off the Via Casilina (SS6). An important Etruscan seventh-century B.C. religious center, Palestrina also drew the Romans, who built the first-century B.C. terraced **Temple of Fortune,** which suffered bomb damage in World War II. The bombing uncovered previously unknown areas of the temple. Though most Etruscan artifacts from the area have been put on exhibit in the Villa Giulia in Rome, there is an interesting museum in the town's Piazza della Cortina.

MANGIARE

At **Labico,** a short drive south from Palestrina, is one of the best little restaurants in Rome's environs: **Antonello Colonna's Vecchia Osteria,** Via Casilina, km. 38.3; tel. (06) 9510032. The 23-mile drive from Rome isn't so very far for a comfortable, elegant evening of dining away from the masses. This old carriage stop has been converted into an elegant restaurant; reservations required. Antonello's *degustazione* special is a gastronomic delight and explains why he is often on call as an ambassador of Roman culinary prowess in presenting the renaissance of traditional recipes in the U.S. and West Germany. Try the ceci bean soup, wild boar. Meals run Lit. 80,000. Closed Sun. evening, Mon., Aug. All cards.

Temple of Fortuna Primigenia, (c. 80 B.C.)

Set into the slope of Mount Ginestro, the grandiose ruins of the Roman Temple of Fortuna Primigenia dominate the town of Palestrina and the surrounding countryside as far as the Tyrrhenian Sea. After the fall of the Roman Empire, the site was gradually covered and only unearthed when an 1944 Allied bombing attack destroyed many of the town's buildings.

Modern day visitors can view the third through seventh terraces of this multitiered temple devoted to the telling of fortunes. These terraces, which echo the contours of the mountain, are unified by a central sweep of ascending ramps. Each level of the temple, however, has its own unique form. Semicircular vaulted and columned niches on the fourth level demonstrate the Romans' ability to combine sophisticated concrete technology with traditional classical decoration. The repeated stalls of the fifth level reveal stores where merchants, such as wine-sellers, weavers, and money changers, sold their goods. The revenues of these shops supported the temple complex. The sixth level originally consisted of a large piazza framed by an arcade. This level now incorporates a broad paved street and a wall revealing remnants of the arcade. On the seventh level, semi-circular concave stairs led up to the culminating circular temple.

The stairs now conclude in the Renaissance Palazzo Colonna-Barberini which houses the archaeological museum for the site. Among the museum's treasures is the *Barberini Mosaic*, a luxurious landscape of the Nile River, which originally decorated part of the third level.

—Mary Beth Betts and Charles Ayes

Rieti. Reiti's province is rich in **religious shrines,** most notably the four sanctuaries founded by St. Francis of Assisi along the perimeter of the Reatina Holy Valley. The **ski resort of Monte Terminillo** was proclaimed by Mussolini "the mountain of Rome." There is no direct rail link to Rome; bus service connects Rieti's Piazza Mazzini rail terminal with the Castro Pretorio and Corso d'Italia terminals in Rome. But since most points of interest are in the province, a car is practically a necessity. Rieti is 48 miles from Rome on Via Salaria.

The geographical center of Italy is in the provincial seat's Piazza S. Rufo, connected to central Corso Garibaldi by Via Cerroni. The point is marked by a plaque inscribed in twenty languages.

The four sanctuaries in the Holy Valley are:

Poggio Bustone, ten miles north of Rieti off SS79, where St. Francis prayed and meditated in two caves.

Santa Maria della Foresta, two and a half miles directly north of Rieti, a stop on the saint's travels in 1225.

Fonte Colombo, three miles southwest of Rieti. Here, in 1223, St. Francis reportedly dictated the rules of his order.

Greccio, ten and a half miles from Rieti at the western end of the valley. In the winter of 1223, St. Francis created the first nativity scene by saying mass at a manger; every year the occasion is commemorated locally with a "living" reproduction of the event on Christmas Eve.

❦ MANGIARE

The town of **Greccio** has the unique restaurant **Il Nido del Corvo,** tel. (0746) 753181. Ample signs from the town square lead to this hill-clinging restaurant adorned with religious artifacts of debatable origin. Outside dining overlooking the valley in summer. "The Crow" greets guests in a straw cowboy hat, Hawaiian shirt, short leather pants, and cowboy boots. His plates of the day are for serious eaters only, with *antipasto,* two pasta or rice courses, two meat or fowl dishes, dessert, wine, coffee, and more. Meals are Lit. 35,000. Open daily. AE, DC.

Sermoneta. The train from Rome's Termini Station to Latina Scalo takes less than half an hour. For under Lit. 10,000 a taxi will then take you, in less than 15 minutes, to the charming little medieval town of Sermoneta, around the 13th-century **Caetani castle.** Castle tours are conducted in Italian from March to October hourly from 10 A.M. to noon and 3 to 6 P.M.; closed Thursday (Lit. 3000). Plans indicate that English information sheets will soon be available. The castle, which briefly belonged to the Borgias, is amazingly well preserved. The town itself is so clean and well preserved it seems more Umbrian than Lazio.

🦋 MANGIARE

A pleasant surprise in **Sermoneta** is Michele Sabba's **Black Rose,** Via G. Garibaldi 17; tel. (0773) 30021. After 20 years in Sydney, Australia, Michele and family returned home to open this pizzeria-trattoria that has everything from hot dogs and hamburgers to meat pies and pizzas from a wood oven, as well as homemade pasta. Going into his second year, Michele hopes negotiations for credit cards will soon be complete. Closed Tues., Jan.

If the sweet tooth is commanding, head for **Engelberto Carosi's ice cream** at Via del Castello 8, just before the entrance to the Caetani castle. There is a little garden with tables; the well—well don't talk about it. While renovating the building Carosi found hundreds of old books and manuscripts that he thought were worthless; he chucked them all into the well. He still has nightmares thinking about their value, estimated by his antique-dealer brother. Two skeletons were found in the building's walls; villagers believe they were victims of Lucretia Borgia, who was given the castle by Borgia Pope Alexander VI when the Caetanis were excommunicated and momentarily turned out into the cold.

Also in the area is the "medieval Pompeii" of **Ninfa,** annihilated by malaria in the 17th century. Nestled along a small lake fed by the Ninfa River, the beautiful little village has botanical gardens that can be visited on the first Saturday and following Sunday of each month, from April through October. Another local attraction is the 13th-century **Abbey of Valvisciolo,** open 8 A.M. to noon and 3 to 6 P.M. in winter, from 3:30 to 7 P.M. afternoons in summer. Visit the spirits shop next to the abbey, which sells liqueurs made by the monks. You'll want a car to visit Ninfa.

Tivoli was to the Roman emperors what Southampton is to New York's investment banking set: an escape from the city. The town is 15 miles from Rome on the Via Tiburtina (SS5). You can take a bus from Via Gaeta near Termini and Piazza della Repubblica.

About half a mile before Tivoli, to the right as you travel from Rome, is **Hadrian's Villa** (Villa Adriana), entrance is Lit. 4,000 (open 9 A.M. to one and a half hours before sunset). The massive second-century complex built by the emperor as his country place consisted of thermal baths and the re-creation of his favorite monuments from sites throughout the empire. One of the most impressive: Canopus on the Nile; Hadrian re-created this Egyptian town with its canal lined with statues and gardens. A fine reproduction at the entrance to the ruins provides orientation, and there's a museum displaying finds from the excavations. The size of the complex is evocative of the grandiose sense of scale of the Roman Empire.

In Tivoli itself is the Renaissance **Villa d'Este,** built by Cardinal Ippolito d'Este in the middle of the 16th century as his retreat. (Open 9 A.M.; evening hours have been suspended, since night lighting is believed to have caused damage to fauna in the villa. Admission is Lit. 5,000.) The gardens surrounding the house present a formidable display of streams, fountains, cascades, and waterfalls against a lush background of greenery.

MANGIARE

Behind Tivoli overlooking the old town is the **Hotel Torre Sant' Angelo,** Via Quintilio Varo; tel. (0774) 23292, a restructured 10th-century castle with pool and private park for its 40 rooms with private baths. There's also a restaurant here. When not hosting political refugees at the expense of the Italian government the rates are Lit. 35,500–52,100. (No cards).

In Tivoli's old town is the **Sibilla Restaurant,** Via della Sibilla 50; tel. (0774) 20281. Sibilla is also the entrance to the Temple of Vesta. Dine on a terrace with a fine view; tables are actually placed among the ruins of the temple, dating from the Roman Republic. Meals run Lit. 30,000–40,000. Closed Mon. AE, DC, V.

Viterbo still has the air of a medieval city. Rail service from Rome leaves from Piazzale Flaminio. Viterbo is 50 miles away, on Via Cassia. A one-hour stroll can take in most of the sights within the walled city, including **Piazza San Lorenzo,** which covers the former Etruscan acropolis; the 12th-century **cathedral,** and the 13th-century Gothic **Papal Palace** where several popes were elected.

TRAVELER'S INFORMATION

For Information Before You Go

Tourist Offices

With more than 50 offices worldwide, the **Italian Government Tourist Office (ENIT)** is the official source of information and advice on planning a trip to Italy. They are happy to provide information, maps, and literature. These are just a few of their locations:

UNITED STATES

New York: 630 Fifth Ave., Suite 1565, New York, NY 10111; tel. (212) 245-4961

Chicago: 500 N. Michigan Ave., Suite 1046, Chicago, IL 60611; tel. (312) 644-0990

San Francisco: 360 Post St., Suite 801, San Francisco, CA 94108; tel. (415) 392-5266

Dallas: c/o Alitalia, 8350 Central Expressway, Dallas, TX 75206; tel. (214) 692-8761

Atlanta: c/o Alitalia, 223 Perimeter Center Parkway, Suite 530, Atlanta, GA 30346; tel. (404) 223-9770

CANADA

Montreal: 3 Place Ville Marie, Suite 2414, Montreal, PQ H3B 3M9; tel. (514) 866-7667

Toronto: c/o Alitalia, 120 Adelaide St. West, Suite 1202, Toronto, Ontario; tel. (416) 363-1348

GREAT BRITAIN

London: 1 Princes St., London W1R 8AY, England; tel. (01) 408-1254

AUSTRALIA

Sydney: c/o Alitalia, 124 Philip St., Sydney, 2000, New South Wales; tel. (02) 221-3620

Melbourne: c/o Alitalia, Pearl Assurance Bldg., 143 Queen St., Melbourne 3000, Victoria; tel. (03) 601171

Communications

Letters

Full addresses are given herein for hotels and agencies in Italy. Writing to a hotel or other establishment for information can take time and be frustrating. Always be sure to send your letters air mail (*via aerea*). Street numbers in Italian addresses *follow* the name of the street. Postal codes (akin to U.S. zip codes) *precede* the name of the city. The names of smaller towns or common town names sometimes are followed by an abbreviated provincial code (given herein in parentheses). A full street address would run like this:

American Embassy, Via Vittorio Veneto 121, 00187 Rome.

When addressing an envelope, set it up like this:

American Embassy
Via Vittorio Veneto 121
00187
Rome (Provincial code here for smaller towns; these are in parentheses in our hotel listings when necessary.)
ITALIA

Post Offices

The main Rome post office is at Piazza San Silvestro in the heart of the monumental area. Hours are 8:30 A.M.–8 P.M. Mon.–Fri. and 8:30 A.M. to 12 noon on Sat. Several other district stations can be found in key locations of the city where packages can be mailed, money orders transmitted and cashed as well as ferma posta facilities, where you can receive mail. The main station as well as the district stations also transmit telegrams and offer public telex facilities. Telegraphic services at San Silvestro are available around the clock.

There are also a number of sub-stations scattered across the city that offer most postal services from 8:30 A.M.–2 P.M. Mon.–Fri., and 8:30 A.M.–12 noon Sat. These can also receive packages for shipping, but district offices or San Silvestro are recommended to avoid unnecessary confusion.

Stamps may be purchased from post offices as well as in nearly every tobacco store and in local bars. Inform yourself about postal rates before purchasing stamps at a tobacconist as they are unprepared to assist on overseas rates. This is important since new rates will be applied in May 1989 and some services (Special Delivery, i.e., *Espresso*) will be discontinued at that time.

Italian postal regulations are quite specific as to how packages must be wrapped, the number of knots in the binding string and type of paper. It's worth the added Lit. 1–2,000 to have the package wrapped by a neighborhood tobacconist offering such services. Those near post offices know not only the regulations but the whims of particular clerks that often give personal interpretation to application of the regulations.

A 24-hour express service exists, but it does not blanket the entire country. It does take in most places on normal tourist itineraries and is an excellent means for recovering passports inadvertently left in custody at another hotel. Average cost is Lit. 20,000.

RAPID CROSS-TOWN DELIVERY

Recent trials by Rome newspapers have set the average time for a letter posted in Rome to reach a Rome address at eight days. Such intra-city postal disservice has sired a number of private delivery agencies that within an hour or two will pick up and deliver letters and documents within Rome for about Lit. 10,000. Several of these agencies that are connected by radio to freewheeling moped riding couriers are: City Mail, tel. 384343; City Service, tel. 7945841; Easy Rider, tel. 5377339; Pony Express, tel. 3309; and Road Runner, tel. 351216.

MAILING LETTERS

Italian mail boxes are red with two slots. On the right is exclusively for Rome mail, the other on the left is for "all other destinations." They are outside all post offices, near most tobacco shops that sell stamps and at various key points throughout the city. At the main Termini rail depot there are letter drops serviced hourly. These are in the mezzanine between the tracks and main body of the terminal near the Via Marsala exit. The only place in Rome where a letter can be stamped, accepted, and canceled by postal authorities at any hour of the day or night (except national and religious holidays) is the registered mail window in a sub-station on Via Marsala in the rear of the main rail terminal.

VATICAN MAIL

As an independent state Vatican City has its own mail system requiring Vatican City stamps. The main post office for those not having direct access to the city-state is behind the colonnade on the right side of St. Peter's Square just up from the newsstand when you're heading towards the basilica. During peak tourist seasons there is a trailer postal facility in the square itself. Vatican letter drops are blue one-slot boxes. It is always best to utilize Vatican stamps for mailings at the Vatican and Italian stamps when utilizing the Italian system, but there is no need to make a trip back to the Vatican just to mail a post card. Neither system has ever been known to destroy mail utilizing the other system's postage. The same tolerance exists that is found with acceptance of Vatican coins in Italy and vice versa. The Vatican has a reputation of offering a more reliable service. Basically it's a question of time in collection considering the size of St. Peter's Square compared to that of the city of Rome. Mailings from San Silvestro, Termini, and Leonardo da Vinci will take the same amount of time to reach destination as those from St. Peter's. After all, it is the Italian postal system that takes in consignment outgoing Vatican mail.

Telephones

The great Rome telephone revolution is in full gear and may well be resolved by 1990 when Italy hosts soccer's World Cup tournament. The demands of the international press will severely test the renovation that has tried the patience of local residents over the past two years. Hundreds of miles of new lines have been laid to allieviate a system that was totally incapable of servicing areas that rapidly evolved from residential to business. It's hoped that the common 18-month wait to have a phone line installed will be relegated to the past.

The most immediate result of the renovation is the change in a number of exchanges in the monumental center and the area adjacent to the Vatican. Serious efforts have been made in this book to provide the most up-to-date information possible. But, unfortunately, some number changes may have slipped through the net. Consult the 1988–89 telephone book, and look for a notation in parentheses: (prenderà . . .); this means the nunber has changed and the number following "prenderà" is the new number. A guide to Italian phone books follows this section.

If your hotel room has a private phone, an outside line may usually be obtained by dialing "0" and the front desk by dialing "9." Telephone units consumed are registered at the front desk and you are billed accordingly, including whatever surcharge the hotel feels appropriate for the service it is providing. For local calls the difference is minimal, but on international—especially overseas—calls, the difference can be enormous; **don't call overseas direct;** your phone bill may well be higher than your hotel bill.

Collect calls cannot be made within Italy, but can be made for all international calls. These must be made through the operator. A collect call is "carico destinatario" or more simply an "R." International operators are "15" for European calls and "170" for other international calls. Most "170" operators speak English. And it is not rare for the operator to ask the number from which you're calling. In such cases you will be called back once the connection has been made. To guarantee receiving the call advise the hotel's front desk before making the call.

If you are making the call from a public phone, be sure the phone you are using receives calls; many public phones are not geared to receive calls. If calling from a nonreceiving phone, inform the operator of such while placing the call and hope the connection will be made immediately.

The availability of public telephones throughout the city is increasing almost daily. Public phones are often found at shops, bars, restaurants, hotels, tobacconists, etc. An establishment that has one usually has a blue-rimmed-yellow sticker with a picture of a blue telephone receiver on the outside of the premises.

Areas of major transit such as air and rail terminals and turnpike refreshment stations will have phones equipped for magnetic cards; such cards are sold for either Lit. 6,000 or Lit. 10,000 by the closest newsstand or cashier. All other public phones are geared for tokens *(gettone)* that are Lit. 200 each—the price of one six-minute local call. After six minutes another gettone is required or the call will be cut off.

Newer phones are also geared to accept coins—generally Lit. 200 and 100 pieces. The most recent models will also accept Lit. 500 pieces. Change is not provided.

Older models have just a gettone slot. A gettone has one track on one side and two tracks on the reverse, so be sure it is inserted properly. Next to the gettone slot will be a button to be pushed only after the call has been answered. These particular models do not return gettone.

More recent models return gettone and as many as 15 may be inserted if making a long distance call. If the number desired is engaged hang up and dial again. It is not necessary to push the return button and insert gettone again. The phone is already geared for making the call. Only push the return button if you are leaving that particular call box or have finished the call.

Contrary to the instructions on the face of the public phone, don't push the return button repeatedly; this can put the phone off balance, and your coins may never be returned. In such cases the problem is between you and the phone company; the proprietor of the premises on which the phone is located is not responsible for malfunctioning telephones.

To properly assure return of coins and/or tokens, hang up, wait about 10 seconds and after hearing a faint "clink" from inside the box press the return button.

If all of this sounds too complicated then utilize the metered call service provided directly by the SIP (Italian Telephone Company). Main facilities are at the Piazza San Silvestro main post office and the first underground level at the Termini rail station. Another is next to the district post office in Prati on Viale Mazzini.

TELEPHONE DIRECTORIES

The Rome network directory (including Ostia and Fiumicino) and accompanying yellow pages are divided into two sections. The first is for A through L and the second M through Z. However, the main directories are not exclusively alphabetical. They abundantly utilizes group listings that can be confusing to non-Italian-speaking visitors. If a listing is not found in a purely alphabetical search, then it must be determined if the listing desired falls into a specific category such as airline, hotel, insurance company, shipping company, restaurant, etc. Then try using the Italian word for the most appropriate category and make another alphabetical consultation with the phone book. For example: if the number of the XYZ Hotel is desired, turn to the first volume (A–L) and under *alberghi* (hotels) and there will be an alphabetical sequence of all hotels in Rome. The same holds for restaurants *(ristorante)*, airlines *(linee aeree)*, insurance companies *(assicurazioni)*, etc.

If lodging facilities are not under alberghi, turn to *pensioni* (pensiones) where there will be a complete listing. For dining facilities it is a bit more difficult since trattoria numbers, though listed in alphabetical order under *trattorie* will usually be listed just with the owner's name. Many of the more economic trattorias are equipped just with a pay phone and these are not recorded in the phone directory.

To avoid total frustration and loss of time ask at the front desk of your hotel for help.

Language

In all of the tourist towns, English is widely spoken. Only when you venture out of the mainstream may you encounter some difficulty. Don't be shy. Harbor your inhibitions and take a stab at speaking the language. Italians are genuine, fun-loving people and will be honored at the attempt.

PRONUNCIATION GUIDE

Vowels	Sound in English	Example in Italian
a	(ah) as in f<u>a</u>ther	casa (kAH-sah)—house
e	(eh) as in b<u>e</u>t	prendere (prEHn-deh-reh)—to take
i	(ee) as in t<u>ee</u>th	libri (lEE-bree)—books
o	(oh) as in b<u>o</u>rder	loro (lOH-roh)—they
u	(oo) as in b<u>oo</u>t	uno (OO-noh)—one
Consonants		
c	before i, (ch) as in <u>ch</u>urch	cibo (cHEE-boh)—food
c	before e, (ch) as in <u>ch</u>urch	cena (chEH-nah)—dinner
c	before a, (k) as in s<u>k</u>y	caro (kAH-roh)—dear
c	before o, (k) as in s<u>k</u>y	come (kOH-meh)—how
c	before u, (k) as in s<u>k</u>y	cura (kOO-rah)—care
c	before he, (k) as in s<u>k</u>y	perchè (pehr-kEH)—why or because
g	before e, (j) as in <u>j</u>elly	gente (jEHn-teh)—people
g	before i, (j) as in <u>j</u>elly	girare (jee-rAH-reh)—to turn

Consonants	Sound in English	Example in Italian
g	before a, (g) as in goal	gatto (gAHt-toh)—cat
g	before o, (g) as in goal	gola (gOH-lah)—throat
g	before u, (g) as in goal	guidare (gooEE-dah-reh)—to drive
g	before he, (g) as in goal	spaghetti (spah-gEHt-tee)—spaghetti
g	before hi, (g) as in goal	funghi (fOOn-ghee)—mushrooms
gn	(ny) as in canyon	signore (see-nyOH-reh)—Mr. or Sir
q	(koo) as in quick	quando (kooAHn-doh)—when
s	between two vowels, (z) as in as	isola (ee-zOH-lah)—island
s	at the beginning of a word, (s) as in sea	sera (sEH-rah)—evening
ss	between vowels, (s) as in sea	rosso (rOHs-soh)—red
sce	(sh) as in ship	scendere (shEHn-deh-reh)—to go down
sci	(sh) as in ship	piscina (pee-shEE-nah)—swimming pool

GENERAL USEFUL WORDS AND EXPRESSIONS

Yes	Si (see)
No	No (noh)
Please	Per favore (pEhr fah-vOH-reh)
Thank you	Grazie (grAH-tsee-eh)
You are welcome	Prego (prEH-goh)
Excuse me	Scusi (skOO-zee)
I am sorry	Mi dispiace (mEE dees-peeAH-cheh)
It's all right	Va bene (vAH bEH-neh)
It's not all right	Non va bene (nOHn vAH bEH-neh)
It doesn't matter	Non importa (nOhn eem-pOhr-tah)

Just a second	Un momento (OOn moh-mEHn-toh)
I don't understand	Non capisco (nOhn kah-pEEs-ko)
Please speak more slowly	Per favore parli più piano (pEHr fah-vOH-reh pAHr-lee peeOO pee-AH-noh)
Please repeat	Per favore ripeta (pEHr fah-vOH-reh ree-pEH-tah)
Sir, Mr.	Signore, signor (see-nyOh-reh, see-nyOhr)
Madam, Mrs.	Signora (see-nyOH-rah)
Miss	Signorina (see-nyOH-ree-nah)
Good morning	Buon giorno (boo-OHn-jeeOhr-noh)
Good evening	Buona sera (boo-OH-nah sEH-rah)
Good night	Buona notte (boo-OH-nah nOHt-teh)
Good-bye	Arrivederci (ahr-ree-veh-dEHr-chee)
Bye-bye	Ciao (chee-AH-oh)
See you later	A più tardi (AH pee-OO tAHr-dee)
See you tomorrow	A domani (AH doh-mAh-nee)

INTRODUCING YOURSELF AND BASIC CONVERSATION

What is your name?	Come si chiama? (kOH-meh sEE kee-AH-mah)
My name is John Miller.	Mi chiamo John Miller. (mEE kee-Ah-moh J.M.)
Nice to meet you!	Piacere! (pee-ah-chEH-reh)
Where are you from?	Di dov'è? (dEE dOH-v'EH)
I am an American from New York.	Io sono Americano/a (for women) di N.Y. (EEoh sOH-noh ah-meh-ree-kah-noh/nah dEE N.Y.)
Do you speak English?	Parla Inglese? (pAhr-lah een-glEH-zeh)
Yes I speak English, and you?	Si parlo Inglese, e Lei? (sEE pAHr-loh een-glEH-zeh, EH lEH-ee)
No, I don't speak Italian.	No, io non parlo Italiano. (nOH, EEoh nOHn pAHr-loh ee-tah-leeAH-noh)

USEFUL QUESTIONS

How do you say in Italian . . .	Come si dice in Italiano . . . (kOH-meh sEE dEE-cheh EEn ee-tah-lee AH-noh)

What does it mean?	Che cosa vuol dire? (kEH kOH-zah vooOHl dEE-reh)
Do you understand?	Capisce? (kah-pEE-sheh)
Is it far?	È lontano? (EH lohn-tAH-noh)
Can I go there walking?	Posso andarci a piedi? (pOHs-soh ahn-dAHr-chee AH peeEH-dee)
Where is the bus stop?	Dov'è la fermata dell'autobus? (dOHv-EH lAH fehr-mAH-tah dEHll'AHoo-toh-boos)
Where is the train station?	Dov'è la stazione ferroviaria? (dOHv'EH lAH stah-zeeOH-neh fehr-roh-veeAH-reeah)
. . . bank?	. . . la banca? (bAHn-kah)
. . . pharmacy?	. . . la farmacia? (fahr-mah-chEE-ah)
. . . rest room	. . . il bagno? (EEl bAH-nyoh)
. . . ticket office?	. . . la biglietteria? (bee-lleeEHt-tehr-EEah)
. . . police station?	. . . l'ufficio di polizia? (l'oof-fEE-choh dEE poh-lee-zEE-ah)

AT THE TRAIN STATION

I want a one way ticket for Rome.	Vorrei un biglietto di andata per Roma. (Vohr-rEH-ee OOn bee-lleEHt-toh dEE ahn-dAH-tah pEHr rOH-mah)
I want a round trip ticket for . . .	Vorrei un biglietto di andata e ritorno per . . . (vohr-rEH-ee OOn bee-lleEHt-toh dEE ahn-dAH-tah EH ree-tOHr-noh pEHr . . .)
From which track does the train leave?	Da quale binario parte il treno? (dAH kooAH-leh bee-nAH-ree-oh pAHr-teh EEl trEH-noh)

AT THE AIRPORT

Flight	Volo (vOH-loh)
Gate	Sala 'dimbarco (sAH-lah d'eem-bAHr-koh)
Smoking, nonsmoking	Fumatori, non fumatori (foo-mah-tOH-ree, nOHn foo-mah-tOH-ree)
The flight number 104 is boarding now.	Il volo numero 104 è in partenza ora. (EEl vOH-loh nOO-meh-roh 104 EH in pahr-tEhn-zah Oh-rah)

AT THE HOTEL

I would like a single room.	Vorrei una camera singola. (vohr-rEH-ee OO-nah kAH-meh-rah sEEn-goh-lah)
. . . double room.	. . . matrimoniale (. . . mah tree-moh-neeAH-leh)
. . . a room with two beds.	. . . una camera a due letti. (. . . OOnah kAH-meh-rah AH dOO-eh lEHt-tee)
. . . a room with a bathroom.	. . . una camera con il bagno. (OOran kAH-meh-rah kOHn EEl bAH-nyo)
. . . a room for one night.	. . . una camera per una notte. (OO-nah kAH-meh-rah pEHr OO-nah nOOt-teh)
. . . a room for three or four days.	. . . una camera per tre o quattro giorni. (. . . OOnah kAH-meh-rah pEHr trEH OH koo-AHt-troh jeeOHr-nee)
Do you have a reservation?	Ha la prenotazione? (AH IAH preh-noh-tah-zee-OH-neh)
I'm sorry there is no vacancy.	Mi dispiace è tutto esaurito, completo. (mEE dees-pee-AH-cheh EH tOOt-toh eh-zah-oo-rEE-toh)
Can you direct me to another hotel?	Mi puo indicare un altro albergo? (mEE poo-OH een-dee-kAH-reh OOn AHl-troh ahl-bEHr-goh)

AT THE RESTAURANT

I would like a table for two.	Vorrei un tavolo per due. (vohr-rEH-ee OOn tAH-voh-loh pEHr dOO-eh)
What would you like as an appetizer?	Che cosa desidera per antipasto? (kEH cOH-zah deh-zEE-deh-rah pEHr ahn-tee-pAHs-toh)
. . . as a first dish?	. . . per primo piatto? (. . . pEHr prEE-moh pee-AHt-toh)
. . . as an entree?	. . . per secondo piatto? (. . . pEHr seh-cOHn-doh pee-AHt-toh)
. . . as a side dish?	. . . per contorno? (. . . pEHr kohn-tOHr-noh)
. . . for dessert?	. . . per dolce? (. . . pEHr dOHl-cheh)

I would like some fruit.	Vorrei della frutta. (vohr-rEH-ee dEHl-lah FrOOt-tah)
A bottle of red (white) wine.	Una bottiglia di vino rosso (bianco). (OO-nah boht-tEE-llah dEE vEE-noh rOHs-soh [bee-AHn-koh])
A glass of wine.	Un bicchiere di vino. (OOn beek-kee-EH-reh dEE vEE-noh)
Mineral water.	Acqua minerale. (AHk-koo-ah mee-neh-rAH-leh)
Sparkling water.	Acqua minerale gassata. (AHk-koo-ah mee-neh-rAH-leh gahs-sAH-tah)
Plain water.	Acqua naturale. (Ahk-koo-ah nah-too-rAH-leh)
Waiter!	Cameriere! (kah-meh-ree-EH-reh)
The check please.	Il conto per favore. (EEl kOHn-toh pEHr fah-vOH-reh)
I did not order this.	Io non ho ordinato questo. (EE-oh nOHn OH ohr-dee-nAH-toh koo-EHstoh)

The Seasons in Rome

Seasonal Temperatures

While Roman weather is mild-mannered on the whole, temperatures vary seasonally.

	Jan.	Feb.	March	April	May	June	July	Aug.	Sept.	Oct.	Nov.	Dec.
Monthly Average Temperatures in Fahrenheit												
ROME	49	52	57	62	70	77	82	78	73	65	56	47

Time Zones

Italy lies in the Central European time zone, which is six hours ahead of New York and Montreal, one hour ahead of the U.K. and Ireland, and eight hours behind Sydney. Italians have daylight savings time, but they "spring ahead" a few weeks earlier, on March 28, and "fall back" a month earlier, at the end of September.

Annual Events

Check the Italian Tourist Office for a detailed list of annual events. Among some of the major offerings are:

JANUARY
Epiphany Fair, at Piazza Navona on the eve of Jan. 5 Rome

MARCH
Mid-Lent Festivities

APRIL
Holy Week Processions, Holy Thursday and Good Friday

Urbi e Orbi, papal blessing "to the city and the world," at St. Peter's, Easter

JULY
Festa dei Noantri, folklore festival of old Rome in Trastevere

Baths of Caracalla Opera Season, through Aug.

DECEMBER
Christmas and **New Year's Festivities,** mostly in the tradition of the Roman Catholic Church

Holidays

On national holidays Italy virtually closes down, with nary a soul in banks, shops, museums, schools, post offices, or public buildings. Be prepared to rest, for you won't be able to do much of anything else, on: Jan. 1 *New Year's Day;* Jan. 6, *Feast of the Epiphany; Ascension Thursday; Easter Mon.;* Apr. 25, *Liberation Day;* May 1, *Labor Day;* June 24, *Feast of St. Peter* and *St. Paul* Aug. 15, *Feast of the Assumption,* Nov. 1, *All Saints Day;* Dec. 8, *Feast of the Immaculate Conception;* Dec. 25, *Christmas Day;* Dec. 26, *Santo Stefano.*

Opening Hours

Opening hours of museums and churches can be whimsical. If you're anxious to see a particular museum or church, check with the ENIT Tourist Office for up-to-date information on hours and holiday closings. Generally, hours begin and end early. Most stores, many churches, and some museums close for a prolonged lunch hour, a tradition in Italy.

Most museums are closed Mon. If you're sightseeing and not attending mass, Sun. morning is not a good time to visit churches. In general, it's best to start your day early, especially when heading for major attractions such as the Uffizi Gallery or Vatican City.

Admission fees are common, but usually moderate: Lit. 3,000–7,000. Some attractions have free admission on certain days.

SIESTA

From around 1 to 3 or 4 P.M. every day, shops, pharmacies, some churches and museums, banks, and most businesses close their doors. Generally speaking, the further north you go, the less drawn-out the lunch break tends to be. This can be disconcerting to the tourist in mid-swing, who'd rather sightsee or shop than eat lunch. Learn to live with it (there's not much else you can do); start your day early, and tour the streets (or take a nap!) if you don't want a protracted lunch.

The flip side to the siesta is that many restaurants close between lunch and dinner. Just as you may have trouble finding an open store in the early afternoon, so you may have difficulty finding food between 3 and 5 P.M.

Packing

Other than an adapter plug or electrical converter for your hairdryer or electric shaver (a shaver will only need an adapter plug), there are no real prerequisites for packing for a trip to Italy. Use common sense and forget about loading your luggage with all but the kitchen sink—if you think it is better to be safe than sorry, you are bound to be sorry when lugging your overloaded bag around.

The life expectancy of high heels on cobblestone streets is less than zero; bring some good walking shoes. Remember that shorts, bare backs and arms, and miniskirts aren't allowed at the Vatican and in many churches and cathedrals. You'll find that in cities, Italians often dress elegantly, so you may want even your most comfortable touring clothes to have some sense of style. Consider packing nicer trousers along with jeans; a basic dress; or a well-tailored jacket.

Binoculars come in handy for a close-up look at frescoes and mosaics on church ceilings. If you're packing a camera, don't worry—major film brands are available throughout Italy.

ELECTRICITY

The current that flows through Italy is 220 volts, 50 cycles. Any appliances that run on 110 volts will need a converter and all equipment must be fitted with a two-pin, round-shaped plug. Come prepared.

Formalities at the Border

Passports

To enter Italy, all you'll need is a valid passport. Citizens of EEC countries, such as France, need only a national identity card. Children under 16 who are traveling with an adult of the same nationality can be entered in the adult's passport. Minors over 16 need special documents. Unless you are planning to stay longer than three months or to work abroad, a visa is not necessary.

Customs

You can bring in as many items for personal use as you like, as long as they are not intended for trade, given as gifts, or sold. Besides clothing and related accessories, personal items include books, household and camping equipment, one sporting gun and 200 cartridges, one pair of skis, two tennis rackets, a portable typewriter, record player, baby carriage, two cameras with ten rolls of film, binoculars, personal jewelry, 400 cigarettes, and no more than 500 grams of tobacco for cigars or pipes. If you are in doubt about other items, check with the Italian Tourist Office.

You may enter or leave Italy with a maximum of Lit. 500,000. To reconvert your lire at the airport, you'll need the original exchange slip from the bank to prove original lire conversion. There is no limit on how much foreign currency you may bring in (which comes as no surprise), but to leave the country with more than the equivalent of two million lire in foreign currency, avoid any hassles by filling out *on arrival* a V2 customs form declaring how much you are bringing in, to serve as proof of import when you exit.

Money Matters

The Italian unit of currency is the *lira*, or *lire* in the plural; the common abbreviation in Italy (and used herein) is *Lit.* Thus, 1,000 lire would be Lit. 1,000. There are a few more zeros in Italian denominations than you probably are used to, so it's wise to sort that out before you start to spend. There has been some talk in Italy of re-valuing the currency and dropping three of the zeros, but so far it's just talk. Bank notes come in denominations of Lit. 1,000, 2,000, 5,000, 10,000, 50,000, and 100,000. Coins come in denominations of Lit. 10, 20, 50, 100, 200, and the two-toned Lit. 500 piece. With the fluctuation of foreign currency, it's impossible to predict rates of exchange. In fall 1988, the U.S. dollar was valued at Lit. 1280, the Canadian dollar at Lit. 1042.35, the British pound at Lit. 2346.25, and the Australian dollar at Lit. 1100. Call any international bank or check the financial section of your local newspaper for current conversion rates.

Credit Cards

American Express once (abbreviated here as AE) was *the* credit card used by all and accepted by everyone. Those times have changed; look for window stickers in shops, restaurants, and hotels indicating acceptance of *Diner's Club* (DC), *Visa* (V), *MasterCard* (MC), and the new *Si* card.

Traveler's Checks

Since traveler's checks are accepted just about everywhere, they are preferable to carrying large sums of cash around. You can cash them as you need them, and if they're lost or stolen, you're insured as long as you report it right away. Buy a popular brand of checks, such as American Express or Visa Barclay checks, to avoid potential hassles.

Wiring Money

The emergency transfer of funds can be a horror story in futility and frustration. The key is in obtaining proper information and taking the right steps at the very outset of the operation. Rapidity means eliminating as many intermediate steps as possible. In the U.S. the transaction can mean using a local bank which has a correspondent in New York, which in turn has a correspondent in Italy, whose main office may not be in Rome. Considering the six-hour time difference between Rome and New York, one Rome bank working day can already be lost in the hassle. To assure the arrival of funds as rapidly as possible have the sender initiate the transaction directly at an American Express office. If in New York the transaction will be direct.

If elsewhere in the U.S. at the least the relay will be through New York. Obtain from the sender all protocol numbers on the operation so they can be furnished to the American Express office in Rome to properly run a trace on the transfer if any bug arises.

Changing Money

As Italian banks become more computerized the differences in exchange rates between various banks become narrower and narrower. But, foreign currency is a market commodity just like potatoes and each bank's supply and demand will dictate its offering price. Quite simply for the average tourist who is limited in sightseeing time the best alternative is to simply utilize a bank enroute on the day's program. There are several on Piazza Risorgimento (end of the line for the 30 tram) between St. Peter's and the Vatican Museums, Via del Corso, Via Vittorio Veneto and Piazza di Spagna, where American Express is also located. Where American Express has been praised for its fund transferring capabilities, it is not known for offering the best exchange rates in town. Italian banking hours for exchanging traveler's checks are between 8:30 A.M. and 1:30 P.M. Mon.–Fri. Italian banks open for one hour in the afternoon, usually 2:45–3:45 P.M. or 3–4 P.M. depending on the bank. Some will refuse to cash TCs during the afternoon opening. American Express will exchange in the afternoon. There are also a number of independent exchange agents around town that are open to 6 P.M. On weekends there are exchange facilities at the Termini station, which offers rates substantially lower than bank rates. The FS facility should stay open to 8 P.M., but when the lire designated for the exchange window has been exhausted the window closes. A footnote to remember is the Credito Italiano, Piazza Navona 45. This bank is open 8:30 A.M.–6 P.M. Mon.–Sat. and openly caters to the exchange market. A valid passport must always accompany every currency exchange operation.

The worst rates are always in hotels and restaurants, which should be relied upon only in an emergency.

When preparing to move on elsewhere, you can convert lire at the airport, providing you can present an exchange slip from a Rome bank testifying to your original exchange.

Tipping

Italians partake in tipping wholeheartedly and seriously; many of their livelihoods depend on it. But don't feel obligated or intimidated about tipping, unless it is a pleasurable payoff.

Hotels tack on a service charge somewhere between 15 and 18% to your bill. In restaurants, read the menu carefully: A supplement of 15% is usually added for service (*servizio*), but some restaurants also list a *coperto* (cover charge). It is expected of foreigners to leave a 5 to 10% tip in addition to the *servizio*, or to tip 15% if no service charge is listed.

Other considerations are: rewarding the chambermaid Lit. 1,000 for each day of your stay; giving a bellhop or porter Lit. 1,500 for each piece of baggage carried; tipping a room-service waiter Lit. 1,000 or up, depending on the delivery; and slipping the doorman Lit. 1,000 for hailing your cab. Your resident concierge is at your beck and call; expect to reward him an additional 15% over the cost of the service rendered. In top-class luxury hotels it is not uncommon to tip the concierge a few thousand lire per day to guarantee service with a smile and some sincerity. Taxi drivers are tipped 10 to 15%; (you can usually just round your fare off to the next highest thousand) helpful theater and opera ushers merit a minimum of Lit. 1,000, and tour guides, about Lit. 3,000.

Getting to Italy

Since air fares can vary so widely, check with a good travel agent and stay abreast of promotional fares advertised in the newspaper or on the radio before buying.

Once ticketing is taken care of, getting there is a cinch. Italy's two international airports are Rome's **Fiumicino** and Milan's **Malapensa,** which handle all incoming flights from the United States, Canada, Australia, and the U.K. During peak travel periods, flights from the U.K. may be routed into the smaller international airports, in Turin, Venice, Palermo, Naples, Genoa, Cagliari, Bologna, Costa Smeralda, Genoa, Rome's **Ciampino,** and Milan's **Linate.**

Health Concerns

Italy is a Westernized country, and you don't need special vaccinations to visit. It offers all the amenities of home: pharmacies are plentiful, and there is an Italian equivalent for just about everything (and indeed, your favorite products may *be* Italian)—aspirin, cough syrup, toothpaste and shampoo, makeup, tampax, contraceptives, and so on. Pharmacy hours are generally 8:30 A.M. to 1 P.M. and 4 P.M. to 7:30 or 8 P.M. Some skip the lunchtime closing, and one pharmacy in the vicinity always stays open overnight. This works on a rotation system, so if you need a pharmacy at an odd hour, check their windows for a sign indicating which one is on duty.

The water is safe to drink (except perhaps from rural pumps), but as in any unfamiliar place, your body may take some time to get used to it. To be safe, drink bottled water.

If the food and water are having an adverse effect on your plumbing system, try squeezing a lemon into a glass of water.

Avis car rental has a service that began in Britain a while back offering renters in Italy access to a 24-hour hotline, *On Call Europe.* For the cost of a toll call, you can talk to an English-speaking doctor or dentist about whatever ails you. Ask about details when you rent your car.

Medical Assistance

In case of absolute emergency have the hotel portiers call the Questura (police) emergency no. 113. The police filter all calls for the Guardia Medica (Medical Watch) with whom they are in constant radio contact. This is the quickest possible means of obtaining competent medical assistance. Doctors are on duty in radio cars in strategic points across the city.

Public ambulance service is administered by the Italian Red Cross, tel. 5100. Response is not always immediate.

Principal hospitals with 24-hour emergency ward (pronto soccorso) service are:

Policlinico A. Gemelli, Largo Gemelli 8; tel. 33051.
Policlinico Umberto I, Viale Policlinico 250; tel. 49971.
Bambino Gesú (Children's Hospital), Piazza S. Onofrio 4; tel. 65191.
Nuovo Regina Margherita, Via Morosini 30; tel. 58441.
Oftalmico (Ophthalmic) di Roma, Piazzale degli Eroi 11; tel. 317041.
San Camillo, Circonvallazione Gianicolense 87; tel. 58701.
Sant'Eugenio, Piazzale dell'Umanesimo; tel. 5904.
San Giacomo, Via A. Canova 29; tel. 67261.
Santo Spirito, Lungotevere in Sassia; tel. 650901.

The above services are suggested only in the case of an absolute emergency especially during the middle of the night. If you do not speak Italian there will be a language problem. All of the above are associated with Italy's social-ized medical plan. EEC-member-state citizens can obtain documentation as to participation in respective plans in country of origin prior to departure on holiday. These certif-icates will be honored in Italy and no payment in state hos-pitals will be requested. Non-EEC-state citizens should have a valid identity document so that you can be billed at home.

Most major credit card companies have emergency medical assistance services that should be investigated prior to departure. The same is true for insurance contract-ed through more reliable auto rental structures.

All embassies and consulates maintain lists of doctors and clinics that they consider reliable. These are not rec-ommendations but lists that will be provided in case of need. On most of these lists is the Salvator Mundi, 67–77 Viale delle Mura Gianicolensi; tel. 586041. In addition to private hospital care, the clinic is staffed by a number of fluent-English-speaking physicians. Out-patient visits may be made either by appointment or going directly to the clin-ic in the afternoon between 2:30 and 3:30 P.M.

A call to the front desk of a hotel for a doctor can at times be adventuresome if not expensive. The fee for the visit often also compensates the portiere. This could open the door to a trail through a medical jungle—especially if being admitted to a clinic is recommended—with wallet-wilting results. This is certainly not always the case, but the possibility exists and necessitates a second of cold-blooded reflection even in the most traumatic moments.

Night pharmacy service is available throughout Rome. Night, weekend, and holiday service is required by law and at least one will be open in every administrative section of the city. As this is on a rotating basis, except for several exclusively night pharmacies, consult with the hotel por-tiere. Pharmacies are also required to post a notice, if closed, indicating the nearest pharmacy that is open. This also holds for the July–August holiday period.

In Case of Loss or Theft

Police reports should be filed at the Questura Centrale, Of-ficiio Stranieri (Main Police Headquarters, Foreigners' Of-fice), Via Genoa 2. Copies of the police report will be issued immediately to satisfy the needs of diplomatic mis-sions, credit card and insurance companies, etc. English speaking police officers will assist visitors. Neighborhood police precincts can accept reports but many have developed the habit of automatically instructing visitors (even those fluent in Italian) to go to the main headquarters to alleviate their own work load. And many of them do not have the multilingual forms that are advantageous when the form is required outside Italy. The central office is open around the clock.

To Replace the Following:

Passport: Telephone your respective diplomatic mission (see Directory below) to learn exactly what is needed to obtain a duplicate and the hours that the office is open. A police report will be required. If you arrive with all the necessary photos, police report, etc., the replacement process will be greatly expedited. The U.S. Consulate will not accept instant photographs.

   Credit cards: American Express and Diners Club can issue new cards to replace lost or stolen cards in Rome. The main American Express office is in Piazza di Spagna. The main Diners Club office is at Piazza Cavour 25 (near the Vatican).

   Master, Visa, Access, and Eurocard are administered in Italy by Servizi Interbancari S.p.A. This national banking group can issue stop orders on lost/stolen cards and notify the original issuing bank that will take necessary steps to issue a replacement card that will be forwarded to the user's official residence. No immediate replacements can be issued in Italy.

Stop order telephone numbers: American Express: Tel. 72282.

Diners Club; Tel. 381841. Bank America—Visa: Tel. 1678-21001. Master, Visa, Access, Eurocard: Tel. 1678-68086.

The first two are Rome (06) numbers. The others are toll-free numbers.

   Traveler's checks. This must be reported to an office or representative of the original dispensing organization in Rome once a police report has been filed.

   IMPORTANT: Prepare a travel diary before departing that contains all pertinent information and numbers of all documents, traveler's checks, and credit cards that you will be carrying. This information should never be carried together with the originals. The same holds for air tickets, which can be easily replaced providing the airline is furnished proper information. If traveling in the company of another person carry your traveling companion's information and have him or her carry yours.

Babysitting Services

If a babysitter is desired during the period that corresponds to the U.S. university academic year and you have a day or two to make plans, call the Rome campus of either Temple University of Philadelphia (tel. 3602583) or Loyola of Chicago (tel. 346001). Young students are often willing to babysit. It is one of the very few opportunities open to foreign students in Rome seeking extra spending money. Both Rome university communities are relatively small and a day or two should be sufficient to find an interested party. The advantage here is having a native-English speaking person care for one's children.

Several commercial services are: Arci Donna, Tel. 316449; Ciliega, Tel. 6275705; Centri di Solidarietá, Tel. 4380321; Lampa di Aladino, Tel. 8870550; Gamma, Tel. 7886558 and Buonidea, Tel. 3279994. Most of the above do not have office hours over the weekends, so again, plan ahead if a Sat. or Sun. sitter is desired.

Laundry

Most major hotels will provide laundry service. There are also a number of laundromats throughout the city *(la-venderia)*. These coin-operated machines, however, do not operate around the clock and on holidays. They are accessible only during regular store hours. Normal fee for a three kilo load is Lit. 10,000 for wash and dry. To avoid wasting time drop off laundry in the morning, be willing to pay a Lit. 1–2,000 service charge, then return before closing time in the evening to pick up your clean wash. If there are wash-and-wear items in your load be ultra-specific about what should not go into a dryer. Many laundromats offer ironing services (for a fee) as well as dry cleaning machines, but don't expect one-day service.

DRY CLEANING

A *tintoria* is a dry cleaner. Make certain the machinery is in-house as many of the small locales are strictly pick-up points that will need at least three days to get the job done. Same day service is *urgente* and often a surcharge is applied. A tintoria can also launder shirts and blouses, but will not accept any other type of laundry.

IMPORTANT. In Aug. it is practically impossible to find a laundromat or dry cleaner open. Those that are operating will be severly tested by impatient tourists. Do not expect same day service. Hotels do not permit individual washing of clothes in the rooms, but an eye is always closed on undergarments, socks, and stockings that have been washed and stretched over the sink to dry. There is a city ordinance against hanging clothes to dry out windows that face a public street.

Business Brief

Italy has been one of post-war Europe's great success stories. Currently, the country is undergoing a major economic boom; doing business in Italy can hold many profitable rewards.

The following are tips on the business protocols of Italy that will assist you in the successful conduct of business with the Italians:

- Northern Italians consider their sophisticated lifestyle to be in direct contrast to the more relaxed southern Italian way of life. Incomes in the North are almost twice those in the South. You will quickly learn that to confuse the two could add both insult and injury to your business relationship.
- Be prepared to use a translator during negotiations, unless you are certain that the person you are conducting business with is fluent in English. Have important documents and agreements translated to avoid any misunderstandings. This could also help to speed up the negotiation process.
- Money is not the only motivation in business. Italians value good relationships with the people they are dealing with.
- Learn to speak a little Italian. This will show the respect you have for the Italian people both as friends and business associates.
- The business day generally begins at 8:30 A.M. and ends around 6 or 7 P.M., usually with a two-hour lunch beginning around 12:30 P.M. Be punctual about your appointments.
- In the past, the head of an Italian firm had the power to make the final decisions. However, today this top-down

management style is being replaced by a more democratic group consensus.

- The Italians are known to be tough, shrewd negotiators. Agendas set for meetings should be flexible and good-faith negotiations are expected. However, it is advised to involve an attorney in final agreements so that terms can be clearly defined and not left in the abstract.

Metric Conversions

Weight			Distance	
1 ounce	28.3 grams		1 inch	2.54 centimeters
1 pound	454 grams		1 foot	.3 metre
2.2 pounds	1 kilo		1 yard	.91 metre
1 quart	.94 litre		1.09 yards	1 metre
1 gallon	3.78 litres		1 mile	1.61 kilometers
			.62 mile	1 kilometer
			1 acre	.40 hectare
			2.47 acres	1 hectare

Temperature: To change farenheit into centigrade, subtract 32 and divide by 1.8. For the reverse calculation, multiply by 1.8 and add 32.

Directory

Tourist Information Centers

In **Rome:** Besides information booths to accommodate new arrivals in Rome in the main Termini rail station, Leonardo da Vinci airport and along major motorways, the Ente Provinciale per il Turismo di Roma (the local tourist promotion and information service) operates an information office for Rome and its province at Via Parigi 5, tel. (06) 463748, behind the Grand Hotel near the Termini rail station. In addition to maps indicating major transit lines and hotel price lists, a wide assortment of pamphlets and brochures is also available.

Elsewhere in Italy: Every tourist center in Italy will have an office in the city or town's rail depot to help find accommodations for new arrivals. Making reservations from another town may at times be difficult, especially if a late afternoon or evening arrival is anticipated. You can, instead, arrive at these tourist information centers, specify type of accommodation and price range desired, and telephone calls will be made free of charge until reservations are obtained. A presentation slip will be prepared complete with the cost of the room so there will be no possibility of misunderstanding. This direct approach may offer shades of uncertainty, but considering the lack of efficiency of the Italian postal system it will always result in shelter and added information for travelers intent on a spur of the monent junket or breaking with a preestablished program after arrival in Rome.

Diplomatic Missions

Australia, 215 Via Alessandria; tel 832721.
Canada, 27 Via G.B. De Rossi; tel. 8840715.
United Kingdom, 80/A Via XX Settembre; tel. 4755441.
Ireland, 3 Largo Nazareno; tel. 6782541.
New Zealand, 28 Via Zara; tel. 851225.
South Africa, 14–16 Via Tanaro; tel. 8449794.
United States, 119/A Via Vittorio Veneto; tel. 46741.

12

HOTELS

Foreign visitors are generally surprised by the high cost of hotels in Rome. Travelers who have not made reservations should consult with the EPT kiosks at Termini or the airport, or turnpike offices near the Roma Nord and Roma Sud exits on the A1 and A2 toll roads. EPT will make phone reservations free of charge; they have information on types of accommodation and price ranges, and will call specific hotels upon request.

Large concentrations of hotels are found around Termini, the Via Veneto, the monumental area of the old town—monumental Rome—on both sides of central Via del Corso (west to the Tiber and east towards Piazza di Spagna), and in the immediate Vatican area and adjacent neighborhood of Prati.

The Termini area is convenient for rail and air travelers. It is also the prime gathering area for illegal aliens, drug traffic, and male, female, and transsexual prostitutes. Various assorted creatures will appear along with the first shadows of evening.

Both houses of Parliament are situated in the monumental area, along with the prime minister's office, many banks, and the best shopping area.

The staid neighborhood around the Vatican is populated by a large number of religious institutes. Adjacent Prati is evolving more and more into a service area, with offices replacing apartment residences due to the law courts on Viale Giulio Cesare and Piazzale Clodio, and many RAI (state radio-TV) offices, stages, and broadcast studios.

The Via Veneto of Fellini's *La Dolce Vita* has long turned to dust. Hookers and hustlers abound amid the tourists and traffic fumes. However, the area still has some fine restaurants and good shopping.

Rates given below indicate the range between single and double rooms.

Credit cards are listed as accepted. "All cards" means that all of the following are accepted: AE—American Express; DC—Diner's Club; MC—MasterCard; V—Visa.

As with priorities, we've keyed hotels into the color map at the back of book, referring to the page number of the insert as well as to the map coordinates at which the hotel is located.

THE SELECTIONS

AMERICAN CHAINS

Three names familiar to North American travelers are Hilton, Holiday Inn, and Sheraton. They have four hotels that are convenient by car off the proper access road from the GRA. None of the four is centrally located, but each will provide bus service to the city as well as the airport.

Cavalieri Hilton   OUTSKIRTS, P. 1, A1
Via Cadlolo 101, 00136; tel. (06) 31511; telex 625337 HI-ROME-I. On Monte Mario, this 387-room, 5-star luxury hotel is a weak financial link in the chain, but is maintained for prestige. (Then came 1988's call-girl scandal.) The pool and La Pergola, a roof-garden discotheque, are popular with Rome's status seekers. The summer salad buffet is actually one of Rome's best noontime bargains (in Trattoria del Cavaliere). All the amenities and a polite, professional staff still make the Hilton one of the best safehouses in Rome for North Americans. Rooms are Lit. 300,000–430,000 with air-conditioning. All cards.

Holiday Inns   OUTSKIRTS
The two Holiday Inns are located at Via Aurelia Antica 415, 00165; tel. (06) 5872; telex 625434; and Via Castello della Magliana 65, 00148; tel. (06) 5475; telex 613302. The first is somewhat near the Vatican; the second is on the approach route to Fiumicino. Both have more than 300 rooms, a restaurant, bar, swimming pool, and tennis court. Both are air-conditioned 4-star hotels with ample parking facilities. Rates in both average Lit. 180,000–230,000. All cards.

Sheraton Roma   OUTSKIRTS
Viale del Pattinaggio, 00144; tel. (06) 5453; telex 614223. This 587-room, 4-star colossus is in the EUR section, east of Rome. Totally air-conditioned, the hotel has large con-

ference and banquet facilities requiring substantial advance booking. There is a pool, tennis court, restaurant, bar, and private garage. Rooms run Lit. 235,000–305,000. All cards.

LUXURY HOTELS

Luxury hotels usually won't accept group excursions, while first-class hotels often aim for that fourth star in order to attract tour operators obliged to book "first-class accommodations" for coach tours. Here are two 5-star, luxury-class suggestions:

Excelsior   VIA VENETO, P. 3, D2

Via Vittorio Veneto 125, 00187; tel. (06) 4708; telex 610232. The CIGA mark is always an assurance. This 383-room hotel across the street from the U.S. Embassy also embraces the famed Doney caffè and piano bar on the Veneto stretch where Marcello Triumphed. One of the first acts of both German and Allied generals when commanding Rome was to require that the Excelsior provide first-class comfort during the rigors of war. Reception and banquet facilities are among the best in Rome. Rooms range Lit. 380,000–542,000. All cards.

Le Grand Hotel et de Rome   TERMINI, P. 3, E2

Via V.E. Orlando 3, 00185; tel. (06) 4709; telex 610210. The 175 rooms of this CIGA hotel are popular with visiting VIPs who don't suffer from hay fever. The ornate trimmings can be havens for dust. Near Piazza della Repubblica (previously called Esedra), the hotel's majestic salons are a desired setting for fashion presentations by leading Rome designers such as Valentino. Rooms are Lit. 350,000–500,000. All cards.

EXPENSIVE

Cicerone   VATICAN, P. 2, B2

Via Cicerone 55C, 00193; tel. (06) 3576; telex 622498. This ultramodern, 4-star, 250-room, air conditioned hotel is one of the newest in Rome. Near the Palace of Justice, it is frequented by Italian businessmen as well as coach tours, who are served by a professional, methodical staff. Rooms are equipped with mini bars and color TVs that receive French and Swiss programs as well as Italian state and private channels. There is a restaurant, coffee shop, and 300-car garage. Room rates with continental breakfast are Lit. 180,000–265,000. All cards.

D'Inghilterra MONUMENTAL ROME, P. 2, C2

Via Bocca di Leone 14, 00187; tel. (06) 672161; telex 614552 Hoting I. This 4-star, 102-room, air-conditioned hotel has been extensively renovated and has regained the splendor that once made this former Torlonia Palace guest house the most fashionable hotel in Rome. Guests have included Mark Twain, Henry James, Hans Christian Andersen, Felix Mendelssohn, and Ernest Hemingway. Valentino is next door and Fendi and Ferre are just around the corner. Rooms are Lit. 233,000–302,000. All cards.

Forum ARCHAEOLOGICAL ROME, P. 6, D3

Via Tor de'Conti 25, 00184; tel. (06) 6792446; telex 622549. This 4-star, 79-room air-conditioned hotel is a fine example of how the Roman ruins were once exploited as a quarry. Wood paneling and marble columns create an on-the-spot and relaxing ambience overlooking the Imperial Forums. The rooms are small, but the roof garden offers the best outdoor dining spectacle in Rome. Rooms run Lit. 210,000–300,000. All cards.

Hassler Villa Medici MONUMENTAL ROME, P. 2, D2

Piazza Trinità dei Monti 6, 00187; tel. (06) 6782651; telex 610208. Next to the picturesque Trinità dei Monti church at the top of the monumental Spanish Steps descending to Bernini's Barcaccia fountain, this 101-room luxury jewel's suites have always been a Kennedy family favorite. The roof-garden restaurant offers one of the best inner-city views of Rome. Thoroughly air-conditioned, the hotel is automatically associated with luxury. Rooms run Lit. 365,000–520,000. AE.

Jolly BORGHESE, P. 3, D1

Corso d'Italia 1, 00198; tel. (06) 8495; telex 612293. This ultramodern four-star, 200-room hotel is geared to efficiency. Air-conditioned, sound-proofed rooms offer refuge from an expressway that runs parallel to the old city walls and from Porta Pinciana, which opens onto the Via Veneto. There are good communications and conference facilities for visiting business travelers, and a restaurant, bar, and parking. Rooms run Lit. 185,000–255,000. All cards.

Jolly Leonardo da Vinci VATICAN, P. 1, B2

Via dei Gracchi 324, 00192; tel. (06) 39680; telex 611182 Jolleo I. This 4-star, 249-room, air-conditioned hotel is one of the latest additions to the Jolly fold. There's a restaurant and bar, plus an unlimited breakfast buffet. Large and small conference facilities are available. The private garage under the hotel was originally built and maintained by a contractor and former owner of the Roma soccer team who sought refuge in England when wealthy Romans were kidnap targets. Rooms are Lit. 173,000–235,000. All cards.

Massimo d'Azeglio
TERMINI, P. 3, E3

Via Cavour 18, 00184; tel. (06) 460646; telex 610556. Oddly enough, not all of the 210 rooms in this 4-star, air-conditioned hotel have private baths. After 100 years a quaint charm of yesteryear still prevails in this corner of glorious 19th-century Rome. Garage facilities are available; there is a bar and restaurant. Rooms with private bath are Lit. 156,000–232,000. All cards.

Parco dei Principi
BORGHESE, P. 3, D1

Via Frescobaldi 5, 00198; tel. (06) 8941071, telex 610517. A modern, 4-star, 203-room air-conditioned hotel with private pool. Almost in Rome's largest park, the hotel is a favorite with entertainers seeking respite from Roman chaos. There is a bar and restaurant, and parking. Rooms run Lit. 199,000–299,000. All cards.

Quirinale
TERMINI, P. 3, E2

Via Nazionale 7, 00184; tel. (06) 4707; telex 610332. Back-to back with the Rome Opera House, the hotel even has its own private entrance that Verdi used when his *Falstaff* premiered in the theater. The Quirinale almost seems out of place on a now-degenerating street lined with bargain shops and second-rate *pensioni*. The barred front door and suspicious night clerk are evidence of after-dark activity in the area. Air conditioned rooms are Lit. 210,000–290,000. All cards.

Raphael
MONUMENTAL ROME, P. 2, C3

Largo Febo 2, 00180; tel. (06) 650881; telex 622396. This 4-star, air-conditioned 83-room hotel is just around the corner from Piazza Navona on a picturesque side street that is usually well guarded, since the hotel is the Rome residence of Socialist leader Bettino Craxi. The machine guns and bulletproof vests detract from an otherwise charming ambience. There is a bar and restaurant. Rooms are Lit. 160,000–236,000. All cards.

Residence Palace
PARIOLI

Via Archimede 69, 00197; tel. (06) 878341; telex 612291 REPALA. In the Parioli residential district, this converted residence was a favorite with the American cinema crowd during the spaghetti-western heyday. The 4-star hotel has 191 air-conditioned rooms, restaurant, bar, large lounges, and a roof garden. The same management has hotels in Naples, Sorrento, and Milan. Room rates with continental breakfast Lit. 106,000–168,000. All cards.

De la Ville   MONUMENTAL ROME, P. 2, D2

Via Sistina 69, 00187; tel. (06) 6733; telex 620836. This 4-star, 189-room, air-conditioned hotel is next to the luxurious Hassler. A restaurant, bar, parking, and courtyard garden make it attractive to its own fashion and entertainment clientele. Rome's leading theater (the Sistina) is 100 yards down the street towards nearby Piazza Barberini. Rooms are Lit. 220,000–300,000. All cards.

Visconti Palace   VATICAN, P. 2, C2

Via Federico Cesi 37, 00193; tel. (06) 3684; telex 622489 VPOLTEL. Completely air-conditioned and soundproofed, this 4-star, 250-room hotel is one block from the Tiber and a 10-min. walk across the river from Piazza del Popolo at the top of Via del Corso. There is a restaurant, cocktail lounge, piano bar, private garage, and conference and reception facilities for up to 200. There's also a roof garden, and some rooms have private balconies. Room rates, with continental breakfast, are Lit. 178,000–256,000. All cards.

MODERATELY PRICED

Bologna   MONUMENTAL ROME, P. 2, C3

Via Santa Chiara 9a, 00186; tel. (06) 6868951, telex 621124 ROMDOM I. This recently renovated 3-star, 118-room hotel in the heart of old Rome, near the Italian Parliament, has a strong MP clientele in the winter; tour groups take the upper hand in summer. Air-conditioning should be installed by 1989. Bar and restaurant facilities. Room rates with continental breakfast run Lit. 95,000–165,000. No cards.

Colosseum   ARCHAEOLOGICAL ROME, P. 3, E3

Via Sforza 10, 00184; tel. (06) 4827228; telex 611151. In a charming area between Santa Maria Maggiore and San Pietro in Vincoli (St. Peter in Chains), housing the famous sculpture of *Moses* by Michelangelo, this 3-star hotel is a 10-min. walk from the Colosseum. All 45 comfortable rooms have baths, but there is no restaurant and no air conditioning. The hotel has a strong entertainment clientele due to special arrangements with a number of Rome agents. Rooms average Lit. 64,000–110,000. All cards.

Columbus

VATICAN, P. 1, B2

Via della Conciliazione 33, 00193; (06) tel. 6865435; telex 620096. This 3-star, 107-room hotel in a renovated 15th-century building is on the main road from the Tiber to the Vatican. The public rooms are well decorated; some are even frescoed. The Columbus has always had a popular following, and reservations should be made well in advance during major religious festivals. There's a restaurant and bar, but no air-conditioning. Not all of the rooms have private baths; but rates for rooms with private bath are Lit. 108,000–168,000, including continental breakfast. All cards.

Fenix

OUTSKIRTS

Viale Gorizia 5, 00198; tel. (06) 850741. This modern, 3-star, 69-room hotel was built from scratch to replace its predecessor. On the park-lined, shaded Via Nomentana, in a quiet area minutes from the center of Rome, it is clean and efficient. The Fenix is benefiting from glasnost; Soviet editors regularly use the hotel when in Rome to discuss business with Italian publishers. Rooms are Lit. 90–137,000 with continental breakfast. Air-conditioning is an added Lit. 9,000. All cards.

Fontana

MONUMENTAL ROME, P. 2, D2

Piazza di Trevi 96, 00187; tel. (06) 6786113. Part of a converted medieval monastery facing Rome's most famous fountain, this 3-star, 28-room hotel has undergone extensive renovation since 1960, when it charged just Lit. 750 for a single with bath. With restaurant and bar (but no elevator), the Fontana's locale is unique, and much quieter now that the fountain's waters are turned off in the late evening and automobile traffic is banned in front of the hotel. Air-conditioning is Lit. 16,000 extra. Room rates are Lit. 66,000–102,000. All cards.

Forti's Guest House

VATICAN, P. 2, B1

Via Fornovo 7, 00192; tel. (06) 6799390. This clean, efficient, 22-room hotel, conveniently located near the Lepanto metro and bus and tram lines, is one block from the Tiber. The evolution of Prati, the neighborhood next to the Vatican, is clearly evident in the Forti's clientele, which include magistrates, actors, musicians, and Italian sales reps. There is an attractive breakfast buffet, but it's not mandatory. Rooms with bath are Lit. 42,000–59,900. All cards.

Gerber
Via degli Scipioni 241, 00192; tel. (06) 3221001. This 3-star, 27-room hotel is on a side street a 5-min. walk from the Lepanto metro stop. The hotel offers a small pergola-covered court and a sun terrace. There is a bar and a restaurant, but no air-conditioning. Rooms run Lit. 68,000–105,000 with continental breakfast. All cards.

Milani
Via Magenta 12, 00186; tel. (06) 4457051, telex 614356. A 5-min. walk from the Via Marsala side of Termini, this clean, comfortable 78-room hotel is used by demanding German agencies for group and individual clients. No restaurant, and the lack of air-conditioning is a handicap in July and Aug. Rates are Lit. 90,000–142,000 for its 78 rooms. No cards.

Porta Maggiore
Piazza di Porta Maggiore 25, 00185; tel. (06) 7004751; telex 612612. This 3-star, 200-room hotel has undergone a thorough renovation. The modern amenities, cleanliness, and efficiency may allow you to overlook the kitschy effort to create an ancient Roman atmosphere in the entrance. Pleasant terrace dining and a solarium are available on the roof. Behind Termini facing the Porta Maggiore, the hotel is minutes from the archaeological zone, the Casilina exit for Palestrina, and the A24 for L'Aquila. Rooms are Lit. 93,000–140,000. AE.

Sant'Anna
Borgo Pio 134, 00193; tel. (06) 6541602. This small, 3-star, 18-room hotel is in one of the most picturesque areas around the Vatican, having survived Mussolini-era rebuilding. Just 50 yards from St. Peter's, the air-conditioned hotel has a charming little breakfast room. Rooms with breakfast run Lit. 95,000–142,000. All cards.

Scalinata di Spagna
Piazza Trinitá dei Monti 17, 00187; tel. (06) 6793006. Just 2 stars and only 14 rooms, all with private bath or shower. This pensione has probably the best spot in Rome, at the top of the Spanish Steps. The courteous, efficient management is an added bonus. The mandatory continental breakfast is served on a roof terrace. Rates for rooms with breakfast run Lit. 85,000–140,000. AE.

Sole al Pantheon,

Via del Pantheon 63, 00186; tel. (06) 6780441; telex 630054. This 15th-century inn has just undergone extensive renovation inside and out and should have a 4th star by 1989. The 28-room hotel is on Piazza del Rotonda, 30 seconds from the Pantheon. A 1513 guest was Ariosto (the author of *Orlando Furioso*), and Mascagni (*Cavalleria Rusticana*) wrote several of his operatic compositions here in the 1800s. There is a bar only, but the surrounding area has an abundance of trattorias and restaurants within a 5-min. walk. Air-conditioned. Rooms run Lit. 125,000–190,000 with continental breakfast. All cards.

Villa Mangili

Via G. Mangili 31, 00197; tel. (06) 3609594. Roberto Anconetani is a young Roman architect who renovated a seedy *pensione* in a turn-of-the-century villa in one of the greenest areas of Parioli. The results are outstanding, and so was the cost. Anconetani and his wife, Luciana, who works with French television, are now majority shareholders of this charming, air-conditioned, 11-room hotel with garden and bar. With continental breakfast, rooms are Lit. 70,000–90,000. All cards.

CULTURAL TIMELINE

Ancient Rome

Aqueducts of Rome, port of Ostia

The Early Christian Era

962	Otto founds the Holy Roman Empire
998	**Monastery of Sacra di San Michele** (near Turin)

The Middle Ages

1000–1150	Romanesque art and architecture at its height in Europe
1063	**Cathedral of Pisa**
1066	Norman invasion of England; Normans also enter Italy
1077	Emperor Henry IV bows to Pope Gregory VII at Canossa
1094	**St. Mark's, Venice,** completed
1096–1291	Period of the Crusades
1140	Guelph and Ghibelline wars begin
1147	Second Crusade
1155	Frederick Barbarossa emperor; struggle between the empire and the papacy
1154–90	Growth of the Italian city-states
1174	**Leaning Tower of Pisa** begun (completed 1350); **Cathedral of Monreale, Sicily**
1209	St. Francis founds the Franciscan Order at Assisi
1228–1253	**Basilica of St. Francis at Assisi;** *frescoes* on the life of St. Francis (1296–1300)
1260	**Pulpit by Nicolò Pisano, Baptistery, Pisa**
1271	Travel by Marco Polo
1280	**Façade, Cathedral of Siena**
c. 1285	**Cimabue, *Madonna Enthroned,* Ufizzi, Florence**
1296–1436	**Florence Cathedral**
1299–1314	**Palazzo Vecchio, Florence**
1305–1306	**Giotto, *frescoes* in the Arena Chapel,** Padua
1308	**Duccio, *Maestà altarpiece,* Siena Cathedral**
1308–1321	Dante, *Divine Comedy;* founding of Rome University
1309–1377	Pope Clement V (French) moves the papal seat to Avignon
1310	**Giotto, *Madonna Enthroned,* Uffizi, Florence;** façade of Orvieto Cathedral
1337–1339	**Ambrogio Lorenzetti, *Allegory of Good and Bad Government,* Palazzo Pubblico, Siena**
1347–1351	Black Death takes 75 million lives in Europe
1377	The papacy returns to Rome
1378–1418	The Great Schism in the Western Church; two popes, one at Rome, the other at Avignon
1386	**Milan Cathedral** begun

The Renaissance (Rinascimento)

1417–1420	Brunelleschi designs the **dome** for the **Florence Cathedral** (completed 1436)
1423	**Fabriano, *Adoration of the Magi*, Uffizi, Florence**
1427	**Masaccio, *The Tribute Money*, Brancacci Chapel, Church of Santa Maria del Carmine, Florence**
c. 1430	**Donatello, *David*, Bargello Museum, Florence**
1434–1494	The Medici dominate Florence (Lorenzo the Magnificent rules from 1469–92); Florence the center of Renaissance humanism
1445–1450	**Fra Angelico, *frescoes*, Convent of San Marco, Florence**
c. 1452	**Ghiberti completes *The Gates of Paradise*, Baptistery Doors, Florence**
1453	Fall of Constantinople to the Turks
	Piero della Francesca, *Legend of the Holy Cross*, Church of St. Francis, Arezzo
c. 1466	**Mantegna, *Dead Christ*, Pinacoteca di Brera, Milan**
1471–1484	Pope Sixtus IV
1473–1474	**Mantegna, *Ceiling Fresco*, Camera degli Sposi, Palazzo Ducale, Mantua**
c. 1480	**Botticelli, *Birth of Venus, La Primavera*, Uffizi, Florence**
1482	Plato's *Dialogues* printed in Italy
1484–1492	Pope Innocent VIII
1492–1503	Pope Alexander VI
1492	Columbus discovers the New World; Lorenzo the Magnificent dies
1494	Medici in exile; Savonarola rules Florence; Charles VIII of France invades Italy; many artists flee Florence for Rome
1495–1497	**Leonardo da Vinci, *Last Supper*, Santa Maria delle Grazie, Milan**
1498–1499	**Michelangelo, *Pietà*, St. Peter's Basilica, The Vatican, Rome**
1501–1504	**Michelangelo, *David*, Accademia, Florence**
1503–1513	Pope Julius II
1505	Michelangelo summoned to Rome to work on Pope Julius's tomb; **Giorgione, *The Tempest*, Accademia, Venice**
1506	Unearthing of the **Laocoön** sculpture group, with Michelangelo in attendance; Bramante begins **New Basilica of St. Peter's**

Index

Mazzini
V. G. Nicotera
'brini Luigi
Avezzana
V. G. Vigliena

Lung. delle Armi
Lung. delle Navi

Via Flaminia

Mus. Villa Giulia
V. d. belle Arti

Gall. d'Arte Moderna
Giardino Zoologi

Piazza Firdusi
Viale del Giardino Zo

V. G. Filangieri
Ministero della Marina

Villa Strohl fern

Temp. d'Esculapio

Viale Giulia

Viale

1

Milizie
Fornovo
Piazza Ponte Cinque Giornate
Piazza Ponte Matteotti
Lung.
V. d. Scialoia
V. d. Romagnosi

Via Pietro Canonica

Villa
Piazza Victor Hugo

Villa
Piazza di Siena
Borghe

Cesare
Scipioni
Magno

Ponte Nenni

Staz. Ferr. Nord Roma Viterbo
Viale Washington

Piazzale Flaminio

S. Maria d. Popolo

Monte

Canestre
Temp. d. Diana
V. W. Goethe

P. Colonna
azza Cola i Rienzo

Piazza
Rienzo
Valadier

Piazza della Margherita
Liberta

V. L. di Savoia
P. za del Popolo

Pincio
V. delle Magnolie

Galoppatoio

V. Cesi
G. Belli

Ponte Margherita

S. Maria d. Miracoli
S. Maria di Monte Santi

Museo di Goethe

Viale

Muro Torto

Villa Medici

Trinità dei Monti

Pinci
V. Pinciana

Cicerone
Tacito

M. Clementi

Ripetta

Babuino

S. Trinita dei Monti

V. Via Lombar

2

cenzio
Op. Naz. Maternita e Infanzia
Casa d. Mutilati

Piazza
Cavour
V. V. Colonna
Palazzo di Giustizia

Via della Scrofa
V. Marzio

Teatro Adriano
Ulpiano

Ponte Cavour
Ponte Umberto I
Ponte S. Angelo

Ara Pacis
Museo di Augusto
Augusto

Pal. Borghese
S. Lorenzo in Lucina

V. Tomacelli

Porta Ripetta

S. Carlo al Corso
S. Croce

Piazza di Spagna
Piazza di Trinite de Monti

V. Frattina
V. d. Condotti
Via Vite

Propag. Fide
S. Andrea de Fratte
Largo Tritone

Crispi

Sistina

Pia

Lung. Castello
Lung. Tor di Nona

Pal. Altemps
Brianzo

p. za Campo Marzio

Pal. Ruspoli

S. Claudio
S. Maria

Via in Via Trevi

Via del Tritone

Pal. S. Agostino

Cam. d. Deputati Pal. Chigi
Piazza Monte citorio

Fontana

Palazzo Quirinale

3

Pal. Gabrielli
S. Maria d. Pace

Chiesa Nuova
S. Agnese
Pamphili
Pal. Braschi
Pal. d. Cancelleria

Piazza Navona

Pal. Madama (Senato)
Pal. Sapienza
Teatro Valle
Pal. Massimo

Pal. Vidoni

Rotondo
Pantheon S. Maria
Borsa

p. za Colonna

S. Ignazio
Coll. Romano S. Maria s. Minerva
Collegio Romano
Pal. Doria

S. Marcello

V. d. Umiltà
p. za

Ss. Apostoli
Pal. Odescalchi
p. za Colonna
Corso
SS. Apostoli

Univ. del Quirinale
Gregor

Maggio

V. 24 Maggio

Pal. Rospiglio

B.
V. Giu

V. d. Pellegrino
Corso
Torre Argentina
p. za Emanuele

S. Gesu
P. za Emanuele
P. za Venezia
Ch. Venezia

Colonna Traiana
Largo Magnanapoli Villa
Foro Aldobran
Traiano

1

0 Viterbo A 1000 Meter B

VITTORIA

Via Trionfale
V. Raffaele Rossetti
Pretura e Corte d'Appello
Piazzale Clodio
Viale Clodia
V.C. di Zebio
Ostiavia
Via Monte Zebio
Via Monte Santo
Via Sabotino
Via Oslavia
V. di Monte Lana

Fedro
Platone
Via Trionfale
Circonval
P.za d. Prati d. Strozzi
Via Angelico
Piazza G. Mazzini
Via Gius. Ferrari
Via Settembre
Via Sette

Viale
Via A. Labriola
TRIONFALE
Via Circonval
Via Trionfale
Via Premuda
V. di Bruno Em.
Faà
Piazza Giovine Italia
V. di S. Pellico
Corte d. Conti
V. A. Baimonto
Via Angelo Brofferio
V.P. Borsieri
V. Damiata
V. Lepanto

Piazzale Socrate
V. A. Labriola
V.S. Tommaso d'Aquino
Mercato
Via G. Telesio
V. B. Savonrola
V. T. Campanella
Largo Trionfale
Giuliana
V.S. de Saint Bon
Viale
Via Doria
Viale
V. Barletta
Viale
delle
Via Legnano
Giulio
Via
Piazza dei Quiriti

Piazzale degli Eroi
Via Cipro
V. A.
Candia
Mocenigo
Leone IV
Viale
Via Vespasiano
Via Ottaviano
Via Silla
degli
Germanico
F. Massimo
Piazza dei Quiriti
Via

Via Meloria
V.F. Albenzio
Emo
Tunisi V.
Veniero V.
Vaticano
Piazza del Risorgimento
Via
dei
Piazza della Unità
V.P. Gracchi
Cola
Via Virgilio

Via Angelo
CITTÀ
Musei Vaticani
Via di P.ta Angelica
Via
Piazza Americo Capponi
V. Alberico II
Piazza Adriana
Cas
S.An

DEL
VATICANO
Pal. d. Governatore
Capp. Sistina
Basilica S. Pietro
S. Pietro
Aula d. Udienze
Borgo
Borgo
Pio
Vittorio
Via d.
S. Maria in Traspontina
Piazza Pia
Via d. Conciliazione
Sassia Vitt. Em.
Pontel.

Viale
Staz. ferr.
Aurelia
Via di P.ta Cavalleggeri
P.za Pio XII
S. Pietro
p.za
Borgo S.
S. Spirito in Sassia
Spirito
Ospedale S. Spirito
Ponte Pr. Amedeo
del Gianicolo
S. Giov.
G. Fioren.
Pal. Sacchetti

Cottolengo
V. d. S. M.
Campi
V. Sportivi
Civitavecchia
Mediatrice
Cottolengo
Gregorio VII
Via di Monte del Gallo
Via Innocenzo III
p.za di S.M. alle Fornaci
Staz. S. Pietro F.S.
Viale
delle
Osp. d. Bambino Gesù
S. Onofrio
Pal. Salviata
Via del Gianicolo
Gianicolo
Lung... Gianicolense
Sansaolo
Ponte

© RV Reise - und Verkehrsverlag, München

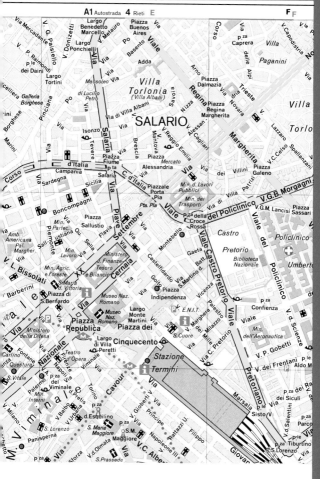

ROME

0	Kilometers	1
	Miles	.5

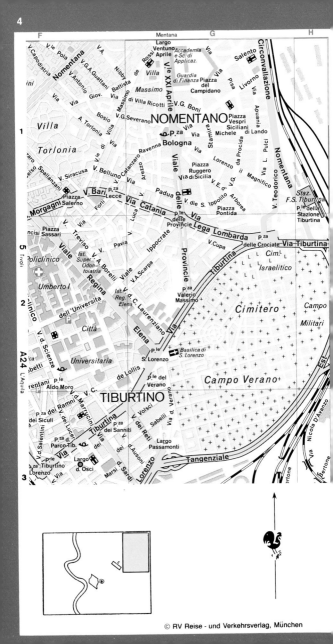

Via
S.Evaristo
p.za Duca Franc. Borgongini
Via
della Cava
nte del Gallo

V.d. Mantell...
Carceri Giudiziarie
Lun...

M. Gianicolo

V.d.S.F. di Sales
V. dei Riari
Pal.
Corsi

AURELIO

Aurelia

Villa

Villa Abamelek

86

Nuova delle Fornaci

p.le 81
Giuseppe Garibaldi

Tor...

V. S. Lucio
Casa del Sole

Civitavecchia

Via

Aurelia

Aurelia
Via
Antica

Villa Medici
S.Pancrazio

p.ta
S.Pancrazio

Aurelie

Villa
Aurelia

p.le
Via
Aurelio

Villa
Spada

Garibaldi

Accad. Americana di Roma

Fabriz.
Ist. Staf.

Medici

I. Quattro Venti
88

Via S.Pancrazio

p.za
Cecchi

Carini

Viale Trenta

Aprile
N.

Viale

TRAS...

Villa Doria

S.Pancrazio

p.za
S.Pancrazio

Vitellia

p.za
Ottavilla

Pamphili

di
Monreale

V. B.

del Vascello

Venti

Bricci

Quattro

Giacinto

Muro

Wurst

Villa
Gianicolensi

Sciarra

Pamphili

Innocenzo

Fonteiano

V. C. Rutario

p.za
Fonteiana

Via

di

Villa

International Hospital
V.G.Rossetti

p.za
Rosolino Pilo

V.F.
Torre

Cavallotti

Poerio

V. Ugo

dell'Onga...

Ba...

Via

Vitellia

Via Pio Foa

Via

V. R. Paolucci

di

S. Calepodio

Cesari

Barrili

V.

A. Mario

Francesco

Largo Bilancioni

Zambarelli

Ozaman

p.za
Donna Olimpia

Viale

p.le
Cecilio Ouinto

p.le
Quattro Venti

V. A.

Viale Villa Pamphili

Guinizelli

A. G.

Largo
Giuseppe Leti

Via

Felice

V.C.Pisacane

V.

Alessandro

Trastevere

GIANICOLENSE

Via F.

V. Fabiola

Donna

A. Toscani

Via P. Fa...

Olimpia

Via

G.

Viale

V. Ponziano

Via

Valla

Parini

Viale

di

Circon

S.Giovanni di Dio Q.

Ghilieri

Gianicolense

Via

V.F.Palaciano

V.A.

Pietro Pignatelli

p.za
Salviati

Cartoni

Largo
Vincenzo de'Paoli

p.le
Enrico Dunant

V. L.

V. Monti

Cir

Gianicolense

Via

G.

p.za
F.Bion...

Staz.
Trastever...

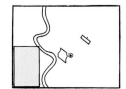

ROME

0   Kilometers   1

Miles   .5

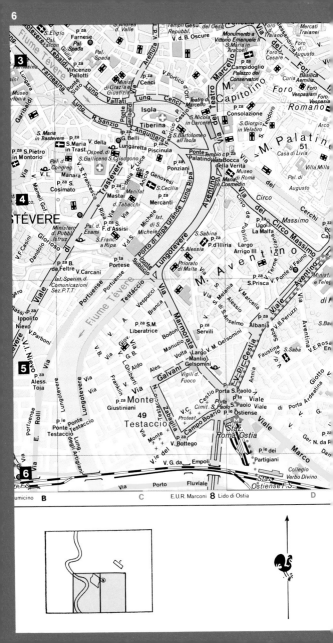

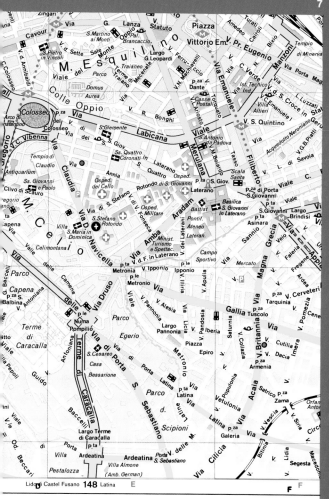

© RV Reise - und Verkehrsverlag, München

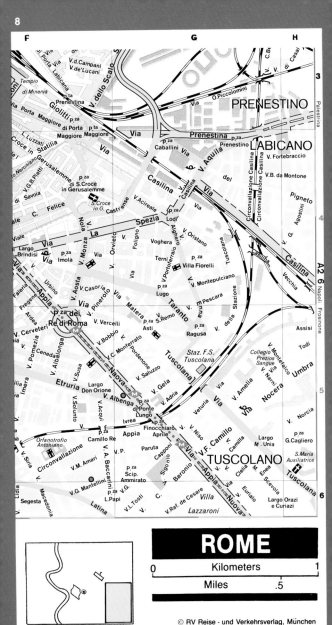

8

F G H

3

PRENESTINO

LABICANO

Pigneto

4

A2 6 Napoli Frosinone

Umbra

Nocera

5

TUSCOLANO

ROME

Kilometers
0   1

Miles
                       .5